CLARE BOOTHE LUCE

CLARE BOOTHE LUCE

JOSEPH LYONS

CHELSEA HOUSE PUBLISHERS

NEW YORK • PHILADELPHIA

Chelsea House Publishers

EDITOR-IN-CHIEF: Nancy Toff
EXECUTIVE EDITOR: Remmel T. Nunn
MANAGING EDITOR: Karyn Gullen Browne
COPY CHIEF: Juliann Barbato
PICTURE EDITOR: Adrian G. Allen
ART DIRECTOR: Maria Epes
MANUFACTURING MANAGER: Gerald Levine

American Women of Achievement

SENIOR EDITOR: Constance Jones

Staff for CLARE BOOTHE LUCE

ASSOCIATE EDITOR: Maria Behan
COPY EDITOR: Nicole Bowen
DEPUTY COPY CHIEF: Ellen Scordato
EDITORIAL ASSISTANT: Theodore Keyes
PICTURE RESEARCHER: Joan Kathryn Beard
ASSISTANT ART DIRECTOR: Laurie Jewell
DESIGN: Design Oasis
ASSISTANT DESIGNER: Donna Sinisgalli
PRODUCTION COORDINATOR: Joseph Romano
COVER ILLUSTRATOR: Kye Carbone

First Printing

1   3   5   7   9   8   6   4   2

Library of Congress Cataloging in Publication Data   90-1098

Lyons, Joseph. Clare Boothe Luce.   111 p
(American women of achievement)
Bibliography: p. 106
Summary: Follows the life of a figure famous for both her plays
and her activities in American politics and government; one of
the first women to represent the United States in a major diplomatic post.

1. Luce, Clare Boothe, 1903–1987—Juvenile literature.
2. Ambassadors—United States—Biography—Juvenile
literature.   3. Legislators—United States—Biography—Juvenile
literature.   4. Dramatists, American—20th century—Biography—
Juvenile literature.   5. Journalists—United States—Biography—
Juvenile literature.

[1. Luce, Clare Boothe, 1903–1987.   2. Ambassadors.   3. Authors,
American]   I. Title.   II. Series.
E748.L894L96   1988   973.91'092'4 [B] [92]   87-34149

ISBN 1-55546-665-6
      0-7910-0419-8 (pbk.)

CONTENTS

AMERICAN WOMEN of ACHIEVEMENT

Abigail Adams
women's rights advocate

Jane Addams
social worker

Louisa May Alcott
author

Marian Anderson
singer

Susan B. Anthony
woman suffragist

Ethel Barrymore
actress

Clara Barton
founder of the American Red Cross

Elizabeth Blackwell
physician

Nellie Bly
journalist

Margaret Bourke-White
photographer

Pearl Buck
author

Rachel Carson
biologist and author

Mary Cassatt
artist

Agnes De Mille
choreographer

Emily Dickinson
poet

Isadora Duncan
dancer

Amelia Earhart
aviator

Mary Baker Eddy
founder of the Christian Science church

Betty Friedan
feminist

Althea Gibson
tennis champion

Emma Goldman
political activist

Helen Hayes
actress

Lillian Hellman
playwright

Katharine Hepburn
actress

Karen Horney
psychoanalyst

Anne Hutchinson
religious leader

Mahalia Jackson
gospel singer

Helen Keller
humanitarian

Jeane Kirkpatrick
diplomat

Emma Lazarus
poet

Clare Boothe Luce
author and diplomat

Barbara McClintock
biologist

Margaret Mead
anthropologist

Edna St. Vincent Millay
poet

Julia Morgan
architect

Grandma Moses
painter

Louise Nevelson
sculptor

Sandra Day O'Connor
Supreme Court justice

Georgia O'Keeffe
painter

Eleanor Roosevelt
diplomat and humanitarian

Wilma Rudolph
champion athlete

Florence Sabin
medical researcher

Beverly Sills
opera singer

Gertrude Stein
author

Gloria Steinem
feminist

Harriet Beecher Stowe
author and abolitionist

Mae West
entertainer

Edith Wharton
author

Phillis Wheatley
poet

Babe Didrikson Zaharias
champion athlete

CHELSEA HOUSE PUBLISHERS

"Remember the Ladies"

MATINA S. HORNER

Remember the Ladies." That is what Abigail Adams wrote to her husband John, then a delegate to the Continental Congress, as the Founding Fathers met in Philadelphia to form a new nation in March of 1776. "Be more generous and favorable to them than your ancestors. Do not put such unlimited power in the hands of the Husbands. If particular care and attention is not paid to the Ladies," Abigail Adams warned, "we are determined to foment a Rebellion, and will not hold ourselves bound by any Laws in which we have no voice, or Representation."

The words of Abigail Adams, one of the earliest American advocates of women's rights, were prophetic. Because when we have not "remembered the ladies," they have, by their words and deeds, reminded us so forcefully of the omission that we cannot fail to remember them. For the history of American women is as interesting and varied as the history of our nation as a whole. American women have played an integral part in founding, settling, and building our country. Some we remember as remarkable women who—against great odds—achieved distinction in the public arena: Anne Hutchinson, who in the 17th century became a charismatic religious leader; Phillis Wheatley, an 18th-century black slave who became a poet; Susan B. Anthony, whose name is synonymous with the 19th-century women's rights movement, and who led the struggle to enfranchise women; and, in our own century, Amelia Earhart, the first woman to cross the Atlantic Ocean by air.

These extraordinary women certainly merit our admiration, but other women, "common women," many of them all but forgotten, should also be recognized for their contributions to American thought and culture. Women have been community builders; they have founded schools and formed voluntary associations to help those in need; they have assumed the major responsibility for rearing children, passing on from one generation to the next the values that keep a culture alive. These and innumerable other contributions, once ignored, are now being recognized by scholars, students, and the public. It is exciting and gratifying to realize that a part of our history that was hardly acknowledged a few generations ago is now being studied and brought to light.

In recent decades, the field of women's history has grown from obscurity to a politically controversial splinter movement to academic respectability, in many cases mainstreamed into such traditional disciplines as history, economics, and psychology. Scholars of women, both female and male, have organized research centers at such prestigious institutions as Wellesley College, Stanford University, and the University of California. Other notable centers for women's studies are the Center for the American Woman and Politics at the Eagleton Institute of Politics at Rutgers University; the Henry A. Murray Research Center for the Study of Lives, at Radcliffe College; and the Women's Research and Education Institute, the research arm of the Congressional Caucus on Women's Issues. Other scholars and public figures have established archives and libraries, such as the Schlesinger Library on the History of Women in America, at Radcliffe College, and the Sophia Smith Collection, at Smith College, to collect and preserve the written and tangible legacies of women.

From the initial donation of the Women's Rights Collection in 1943, the Schlesinger Library grew to encompass vast collections documenting the manifold accomplishments of American women. Simultaneously, the women's movement in general and the academic discipline of women's studies in particular also began with a narrow definition and gradually expanded their mandate. Early causes such as woman suffrage and social reform, abolition and organized labor were joined by newer concerns such as the history of women in business and the professions and in politics and government; the study of the family; and social issues such as health policy and education.

Women, as historian Arthur M. Schlesinger, jr., once pointed out, "have constituted the most spectacular casualty of traditional history. They have made up at least half the human race, but you could never tell that by looking at the books historians write." The new breed of historians is remedying that omission. They have written books about immigrant women and about working-class women who struggled for survival in cities and about black women who met the challenges of life in rural areas. They are telling the stories of women who, despite the barriers of tradition and economics, became lawyers and doctors and public figures.

The women's studies movement has also led scholars to question traditional interpretations of their respective disciplines. For example, the study of war has traditionally been an exercise in military and political analysis, an examination of strategies planned and executed by men. But scholars of women's history have pointed out that wars have also been periods of tremendous change and even opportunity for women, because the very absence of men on the home front enabled them to expand their educational, economic, and professional activities and to assume leadership in their homes.

The early scholars of women's history showed a unique brand of courage in choosing to investigate new subjects and take new approaches to old ones. Often, like their subjects, they endured criticism and even ostracism by their academic colleagues. But their efforts have unquestionably been worthwhile, because with the publication of each new study and book another piece of the historical patchwork is sewn into place, revealing an increasingly comprehensive picture of the role of women in our rich and varied history.

Such books on groups of women are essential, but books that focus on the lives of individuals are equally indispensable. Biographies can be inspirational, offering their readers the example of people with vision who have looked outside themselves for their goals and have often struggled against great obstacles to achieve them. Marian Anderson, for instance, had to overcome racial bigotry in order to perfect her art and perform as a concert singer. Isadora Duncan defied the rules of classical dance to find true artistic freedom. Jane Addams had to break down society's notions of the proper role for women in order to create new social institutions, notably the settlement house. All of these women had to come to terms both with themselves and with the world in which they lived. Only then could they move ahead as pioneers in their chosen callings.

Biography can inspire not only by adulation but also by realism. It helps us to see not only the qualities in others that we hope to emulate, but also, perhaps, the weaknesses that made them "human." By helping us identify with the subject on a more personal level they help us to feel that we, too, can achieve such goals. We read about Eleanor Roosevelt, for instance, who occupied a unique and seemingly enviable position as the wife of the president. Yet we can sympathize with her inner dilemma: an inherently shy woman, she had to force herself to live a most public life in order to use her position to benefit others. We may not be able to imagine ourselves having the immense poetic talent of Emily Dickinson, but from her story we can understand the challenges faced by a creative woman who was expected to fulfill many family responsibilities. And though few of us will ever reach the level of athletic accomplishment displayed by Wilma Rudolph or Babe Zaharias, we can still appreciate their spirit, their overwhelming will to excel.

A biography is a multifaceted lens. It is first of all a magnification, the intimate examination of one particular life. But at the same time, it is a wide-angle lens, informing us about the world in which the subject lived. We come away from reading about one life knowing more about the social, political, and economic fabric of the time. It is for this reason, perhaps, that the great New England essayist Ralph Waldo Emerson wrote, in 1841, "There is properly no history: only biography." And it is also why biography, and particularly women's biography, will continue to fascinate writers and readers alike.

CLARE BOOTHE LUCE

Clare Boothe Luce prepares for a flight in a Navy torpedo bomber. She traveled to Burma in 1942 to report on World War II for Life *magazine.*

ONE

Battlefront Reporter

A few months after the United States entered World War II, Clare Boothe Luce traveled to the Far East as a war correspondent for *Life* magazine. On Easter Sunday, April 5, 1942, the 39-year-old writer arrived in Lashio, Burma, the scene of some of the Pacific front's most heated combat. The Japanese had invaded the region and were rapidly gaining ground against the nation's British, Chinese, and American defenders. Luce's flight into Burma had been a turbulent one, and all six of her fellow passengers, Chinese soldiers on their way to the battlefield, had succumbed to airsickness. Touching down after what she later called the "most gruesome airplane trip I have ever taken in all my life," Luce immediately headed over to the city's Allied military headquarters.

If Luce had expected a warm reception, she was soon disappointed. She sought out the commander of the American forces in the region, Major General Joseph Stilwell, a man known to his troops as "Vinegar Joe." According to Luce's account of their first meeting, Stilwell lived up to his hard-boiled nickname:

> I insinuated myself into the upflowing stream of officers, Chinese and American, who were clumping up and down stairs. I found General Stilwell leading a Sino-American flight of officers down. He was wearing an overseas cap on his close-cropped, grizzled hair, smoking his interminable cigarette in its long black holder and chewing gum rapidly. "Hello, hello," he said brusquely, "Burma is no place for a woman." I started to give him an argument but he was already half down the stairs.

13

U.S. general Joseph Stilwell (left) surveys the position of enemy Japanese troops. Stilwell told Luce that "Burma is no place for a woman."

Undaunted by Stilwell's discouraging words, Luce was ready before dawn the next morning to accompany the general to the American headquarters in the city of Maymyo. Later that afternoon she and *Life* photographer George Rodger visited Mandalay, the scene of a recent Japanese attack. Luce was horrified by what she saw there: The once stately city, celebrated in poetry and famous for its exquisite Buddhist temples, had been reduced to a smoking ruin. Bodies littered what were left of the city's streets and floated in the moat that surrounded an ancient palace. Overcome by the carnage, Luce wrote that "neither Rodger nor I pointed a camera at these fearful indecencies."

Two days later the Japanese attacked Maymyo. Along with the others at the base, Luce huddled in a trench as bombs rained down around her. She had weathered air attacks before, but many of the soldiers at Maymyo had not. She later wrote about their reactions:

> The officers who had their first baptism by bomb were quite different men now. They were smiling, yes. They kidded a bit, but they were not really gay anymore and as you looked from one face to another you saw that they knew at last that they lived in a world where men are mortal. Until you have heard death scream in a shell or bomb through the insensible air, impersonally seeking you out personally, you never quite believe that you are mortal.

When the bombing ceased, Luce brushed most of the mud off her clothing and went to have lunch with Sir Harold Alexander, a British commander who was working with the Americans and Chinese to stave off the Japanese attack on Burma. Luce was struck by the odd contradiction between the Allies' difficult position and the elegance that the general and his fellow Britons insisted on maintaining

Documenting the horrors of war, Luce photographs a wounded Burmese boy. Her vivid World War II reportage enthralled and educated the American public.

even in the toughest of circumstances. Over a cocktail that contained ice—a rare commodity at the battlefront—Alexander glossed over the dangers of their situation. The next day brought more Japanese bombs, but that evening Luce attended a grand party at the Maymyo Country Club. As her biographer Stephen Shadegg wrote, "Her British hosts managed to give everyone there the impression that all was well—the air raids nothing much."

The next morning Clare Luce learned that the Allies, unable to hold back the Japanese much longer, were making plans to retreat. As a civilian, she would have to make her own way out of Burma. If she could not find a pilot willing to bend the rules and take her, she would have to follow a dangerous land route out of the war zone. Before she left Allied headquarters, one of the officers gave her a pistol, accompanied by stern instructions to save a

This Baptist church was one of the few buildings left standing after the Japanese bombed the Burmese city of Mandalay in 1942. Luce was shocked by the destruction.

bullet for herself if capture seemed inevitable.

Luce refused to give way to the growing panic. As she later reported in *Life*, she arrived at the airstrip, found a pilot on his way to China, and proceeded to exert her charm. "I am a lady in distress," she told him, "which I gather is your specialty." "Well, beautiful," he responded, "if you are in distress it's probably your own damn fault for being in China. What am I supposed to do?" Luce asked him to squeeze her onto his overcrowded plane, and the pilot asked her if she had a ticket. "Obviously not," she replied, "or I wouldn't be in distress." Luce's succinct response won her a seat on one of the last planes out of the war zone. The Japanese captured the airfield one hour after her plane departed.

Clare Boothe Luce, already a renowned editor and playwright before she became a war reporter, would have several more careers after she returned from the World War II battlefront. She went on to become a congresswoman, a screenwriter, and a diplomat. With each career change, she broke new ground both for herself

Luce chats with an American soldier. When the Allies withdrew from Burma, Luce had to rely on her wits to get out of the country before the Japanese seized control.

and for all women. As her friend Wilfrid Sheed observed, "Clare was a pioneer not just during office hours but every breathing minute." Born into a struggling middle-class family, she evolved into one of her era's most prominent women. In 1945, *Vogue* magazine compared her to a modern-day Cinderella, a "small-town girl who made good without the glass slipper—just work and push."

Five-year-old Clare Boothe stands beside her brother, David. Born into a stage family in 1903, young Clare led an unorthodox but basically happy life.

TWO

Arranging Clare's Life

Clare Boothe was born into a New York City stage family on March 10, 1903. Her father, William Boothe, came from a line of respectable Baptist ministers. Much to the chagrin of his parents, he decided to pursue a career as a musician instead of following in his family's footsteps. Although he had a fine musical talent, his roving eye and wandering spirit made it hard for him to find steady work. In his mid-thirties he finally settled into playing the violin in the orchestra of a touring musical revue.

At the age of 40 William Boothe divorced his first wife to marry a beautiful woman in the show's chorus, Anna Clara Snyder, who went by the stage name of Ann Clare. A son, named David, was born in 1902, and Clare, their only other child, was born the following year. Family photographs show Clare as an attractive child, blue-eyed and blonde.

According to an intimate account of her life written by her friend Wilfrid Sheed, Clare Boothe Luce's youth was generally happy yet chaotic. The family was always on the move, traveling with touring musicals. The two children often bathed in hotel sinks, and their dinners were likely to center around the cheapest vegetable available, cabbage. After a few years William Boothe decided to drop out of the uncertain theatrical life and managed a soft-drink bottling company in Nashville, Tennessee. When he got tired of that, he signed on as first violin for the Chicago Opera Company.

As for education, the two children took what they could get as they moved from town to town. Clare made up for her lack of regular schooling by reading.

In this photograph of the Boothe clan, Clare's father, William, stands third from the right, between his first wife and his parents.

She owed her determination to learn on her own to her father, who encouraged her to read voraciously and study foreign languages. According to Sheed's account, "If he hadn't, nobody else would have." Ann Boothe's contribution, on the other hand, was to foster her daughter's ambition and confidence. She seemed to pin all her aspirations on her pretty, bright daughter—an attitude that may have been discouraging for her son, David. Later in life, while Clare went from one stunning achievement to another, her brother faded into the shadows, a rebellious and unhappy boy who never found his place.

Clare's unusual childhood became even more unstable in 1912. That year history repeated itself when William Boothe deserted the family to run off with a young actress. Because Ann Boothe could not possibly support her two children on the money she might earn as an actress, the three of them moved into her parents' home in Hoboken, New Jersey. Old-fashioned German immigrants, the Snyders were unhappy that their daughter had become an actress and then married a man of whom they disapproved. Clare Boothe Luce's memories of this period of her life were mostly of the contrast between her grandparents' sternness and her mother's energetic optimism.

Grandfather Snyder died later that year, and Mrs. Boothe and her two children returned to New York City. They moved into a dingy boardinghouse where Ann Boothe did her best to approximate normal family life. As Luce remarked in later years, "Mother always cooked fried eggs by opening the gas jet over the radiator and keeping the window open so the landlord wouldn't smell her cooking and throw us out."

Filled with glorious plans for her daughter, Ann Boothe was one of the earliest "stage mothers," women who devote their life to making their children stars. The New York theater presented all sorts of opportunities. Even better, the studios of an exciting new medium—the movies—were not far away in the suburbs of Long Island and New Jersey.

Mrs. Boothe learned that a rising young dramatic actress named Mary Pickford (soon to become "America's Sweetheart," one of the great stars of silent films) was playing a child's role in a stage production called *A Good Little Devil*. With her mother's help, Clare secured a temporary job as Pickford's understudy. She then won a bit part in another play and appeared in

Anna Clara Snyder, who went by the name Ann Clare, was William Boothe's second wife. The former actress harbored stage aspirations for her daughter Clare.

one of the silent films that were then being produced in Fort Lee, New Jersey. For a while it seemed that her acting career was off to a good start.

Perhaps family history had something to do with Ann Boothe's plans for her daughter. Aside from William

This photograph of Clare Boothe was taken around 1912, the year that William Boothe deserted his wife and children to pursue a relationship with a young actress.

Boothe, there were other theatrical models in Clare's family background. Her granduncle Edwin Booth was considered by many to be the greatest Shakespearean actor of the 19th century. His brother, John Wilkes Booth, was also an actor, although he is better known as the man who assassinated President Abraham Lincoln. (Clare's grandfather may have added the *e* to the family name to distance the Boothes from their notorious ancestor.) But Clare herself, in her own words, was "easily one of the worst natural talents in the business." She had many abilities, as her later life would demonstrate, but acting was not one of them.

Ann and William Boothe were divorced in 1913. According to Clare Luce's account, neither she nor David knew about this event until years later. Ashamed of the circumstances surrounding her husband's departure, Ann Boothe had told her children he was dead. Clare and David later learned the truth, although William Boothe, who had moved to California to establish a music school, remained aloof from the family. He occasionally sent his ex-wife money, much of which went to pay David's tuition at military school. When William Boothe ran into financial difficulties years later, Clare Luce began to send him money and continued to do so until he died when she was in her twenties.

Following the breakup of her mar-

Mary Pickford (seated) appears in A Good Little Devil. *Clare's short-lived career as a child actress began when she served as Pickford's understudy for this play.*

riage, Ann Boothe began to date a tire merchant named Joseph Jacobs, who had made a great deal of money in the stock market. Jacobs instructed Clare's mother in the fine art of trading in stocks. His advice must have been valuable, for Clare and Ann Boothe were able to afford a trip to France in 1914. After six months in Paris, where Clare soaked up the culture and learned to speak the language fairly well, the outbreak of World War I drove them back to the United States.

Ann Boothe had taken her daughter on this jaunt for educational reasons, but she was less interested in stimu-lating Clare's mind than in helping her acquire the sophisticated veneer that would enable her to marry a wealthy, socially prominent man. Now that Mrs. Boothe had given up the idea of a stage career for her daughter, a "good marriage" was the only other future she could envision for a bright, ambitious, pretty girl. Clare, for her part, preferred reading to socializing and aspired to a writing career. In a rare act of rebellion, she sent a plaintive letter to English novelist and playwright W. Somerset Maugham, asking for career guidance and complaining that her mother did not understand her.

William Boothe divorced Clare's mother in 1913, but the children did not learn this fact until years later. Ann Boothe had told them that their father was dead.

Twelve-year-old Clare began regular schooling in 1915, when she was sent to the Cathedral School of St. Mary, an upper-middle-class girls' boarding school in Garden City, Long Island. Because of her unusual upbringing, she was more at ease with adults than with her peers, an attitude that many of her classmates mistook for snobbishness. In time, however, some of the other girls recognized her as a born leader with a remarkable wit that her friend Helen Lawrenson later called "one of the fastest, trigger-quick." She soon built a reputation as a champion swimmer and the most talented writer in her class.

When Clare started at St. Mary's, she was a chubby girl with lovely blue eyes. Her weight problem was a legacy of her unsettled early childhood. As Luce later told an interviewer, "When I was a child, I was so lonely I became a compulsive eater." Clare would struggle with her weight throughout her adolescence; the 5-foot-6-inch teenager sometimes weighed as much as 160 pounds.

Despite insecurities about her looks and home life, she was much more independent than most of her classmates. Her years of reading and travel paid off when she entered St. Mary's and was placed in the eighth grade. All the other girls had the benefit of moneyed homes and solid educational backgrounds, but Clare, with her curious mixture of strengths, nonetheless managed to be first in her class.

At school Clare became close friends with Elizabeth "Buffy" Cobb. She was the daughter of Irvin S. Cobb, at that time perhaps the best-known humor writer in America. Visits to Buffy's house brought Clare her first chance to meet some leading figures of the theatrical and literary scene. A stream of celebrities visited the Cobbs, and the teenaged Clare found that she had the gift of getting along with adults who were known for their wit and charm—people such as theatrical producer Flo Ziegfeld and comedienne Fanny Brice, novelists Booth Tarkington and Kathleen Norris, and war correspondent Richard Harding Davis.

After two years at St. Mary's, Clare transferred to the Castle School in Tarrytown, New York, where she entered 10th grade in 1917, just as the United States entered World War I. By this time Ann Boothe had settled into a comfortable house near Greenwich, Connecticut, and so for the first time Clare had a house to which she could invite her friends for weekends. Her mother's continuing successes on the stock market enabled Clare to dress as well as any of her classmates, a matter that was, unfortunately, of primary interest to many of the students at Castle. A more positive influence was Cassity Mason, the school's headmistress, who maintained that women were the intellectual equals of men and encouraged her pupils to strive for their goals, regardless of sexual stereotypes.

Spurred on by this supportive, challenging environment, Clare soon landed the position of editor of the school paper, a natural reward for the writing skills she had developed over the past several years. She was now focusing on writing plays and poetry and was spending much of her spare

Clare (right) and a fellow student model their costumes for a school play. Thrilled to begin her formal education, Clare quickly rose to the head of her class.

time in New York seeing Broadway shows. She grew increasingly confident as she lost weight and racked up academic and social achievements. At the end of her first year at the Castle School the class yearbook boasted of her, "Yes, she is our prodigy and our genius."

World War I became a reality for Clare when her 16-year-old brother,

Comedian Fanny Brice displays an egg bearing her image. Clare met stars such as Brice at the home of her friend Elizabeth, the daughter of humor writer Irvin S. Cobb.

Clare Boothe strikes a theatrical pose. Although she had no ambitions as an actress, the teenaged Clare was fascinated by the theater, which she often attended.

David, lied about his age and signed on with the Marine Corps for a tour of duty in France. Clare contributed to the war effort by volunteering for the Red Cross, and she wrote to her brother often. David Boothe returned after a few months of combat duty overseas because the United States was only engaged in World War I for a little over a year, but his limited war experience had given him a taste for flying—a fact that would determine his later career.

Clare was offered the chance to skip

a year of school and so was able to graduate at the age of 16 in June 1919. Although her formal schooling had only lasted four years, she graduated first in her class. She had already led a more varied, independent life than most of her peers, and she continued to pursue that course. An avid swimmer, she tried out for the U.S. Olympic team. She came close but did not make the final cut.

Her next move was to leave her mother's house and strike out on her own in New York City. With no marketable skills to offer, the best job she could find was a position making paper flowers and party favors on a factory assembly line. Her salary was low, the hours long, and the work monotonous. Nonetheless, she found herself a room to live in and lasted three months before an attack of appendicitis sent her back home and to the hospital.

The surgery was performed by a local Connecticut surgeon, Dr. Albert Austin. Not long afterward, Austin operated on Clare's mother for the same ailment. His interest in his attractive 38-year-old patient became more than professional, and he soon proposed marriage. A responsible, unemotional man, Dr. Austin brought stability to his wife and stepchildren, but Clare Luce later characterized him as "New England cold."

Clare tried her hand at secretarial school but found that it bored her— writing was still her favorite pursuit. Some of the poems she wrote during this period reflect her early political views, a blend of idealism and toughness that would distinguish her opinions throughout her lifetime. One of them chided U.S. president Woodrow Wilson for his inability to make good on his promise to get the United States involved in the new international peacekeeping body, the League of Nations. "Well, you had not the steel strength in your soul," Clare wrote, "it was too soft to realize the goal. . . .

Hostess Elsa Maxwell serenades musician José Melis. Maxwell was one of the prominent people that Clare Boothe met during her voyage home from Europe.

The dream as such, is still a splendid dream/it's for our shattered hopes in you we grieve."

When Dr. Austin went to Germany to study new advances in plastic surgery, he brought Clare and her mother along. On their first trip abroad in 1914, Ann and Clare Boothe had been ordinary middle-class tourists. But thanks to Dr. Austin's prominence, their 1920 departure was a news event in Connecticut. The family traveled first class, and in Europe they socialized with leaders of the arts and professions. In addition, they had American dollars to

Clare Boothe had grown into a beautiful young woman by the time she traveled to Europe with her mother and stepfather in 1920.

spend at a time when Germany was suffering from terrible inflation. In Berlin, for example, they stayed at the city's best hotel for less than three dollars a day.

Seventeen-year-old Clare had a glorious time during her stay abroad. She returned to all the museums and cathedrals that she had glimpsed only briefly on her earlier trip. She was growing into a lovely young woman and even won a beauty contest on the Riviera. The last leg of the journey was England, where she met Major Julian

Simpson, a British war hero who shared her devotion to writing. Although they had only four days together before Clare sailed home, she suspected she had met the man she would marry. When they parted, he promised to visit her in Connecticut.

The voyage home, again first class on a luxury liner, gave her an opportunity to become acquainted with some of her illustrious fellow passengers. It may be, as biographer Wilfrid Sheed suggested, that the introductions came about because her ambitious mother bribed a steward to change the placement of their deck chairs. In any case, Clare soon became good friends with Max Reinhardt, the foremost theatrical producer of the day; with Elsa Maxwell, whose professional specialty was giving parties; and most important, with social reformer Alva Ertskin Belmont.

Belmont was one of the richest women in America and a prominent figure in "high society." She was also very active in national politics and one of the leaders of the American feminist movement. As a result of the efforts of women such as Belmont, the 19th Amendment to the Constitution had granted women the vote that same year.

That Clare had been a feminist since her school days impressed Alva Belmont as much as Clare's intelligence did. Belmont and some of her supporters were planning to form a new political group, to be called the Women's National party, which would promote female candidates for political offices all over the country. Clare was interested in the group but did not commit herself to joining.

Not long after their boat docked, Dr. and Mrs. Austin received a letter from Major Simpson asking permission to call on their daughter. A few months later he arrived at the doorstep of their modest frame house. He spent an uncomfortable two days, left hurriedly, and promised to write. He never did. A friend in England finally explained that the major was poor and deeply in debt. He had hoped to marry into wealth and had been very disappointed to discover that Clare was not, as he had believed, a rich American heiress.

Clare soon got over this painful rejection; perhaps she even learned something from it. For even as a teenager, she seemed determined to overcome all setbacks in order to make her mark on the world—although at this point she was not sure how she would accomplish that goal. Certainly Alva Belmont saw a bright future ahead for young Clare Boothe. In a letter that would prove prophetic, she wrote a friend that she had "met a girl on the boat who has all the earmarks of talent and success. She's only seventeen and she's poor, but she has beauty and brains to go as far as her ambition will take her."

Clare Boothe strolls the deck of an ocean liner with her ambitious mother, who was grooming her daughter for a socially and financially advantageous marriage.

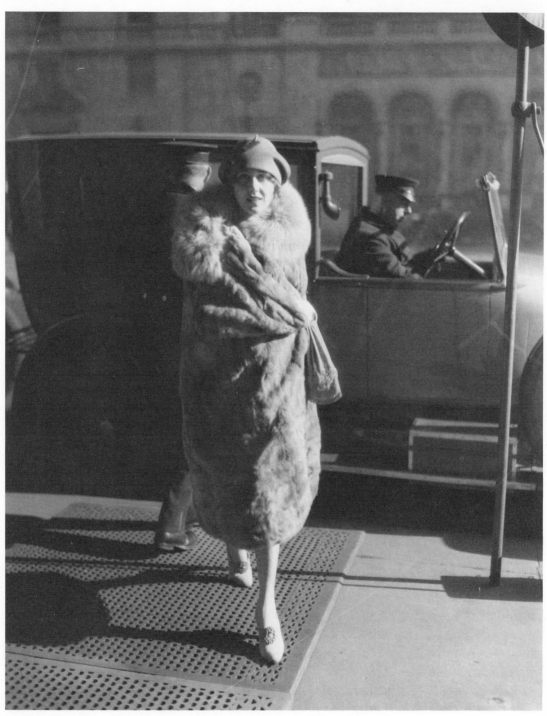

Swathed in furs, Clare Boothe Brokaw steps out of her limousine in 1924, a year after she married the wealthy George Brokaw.

THREE

Marriage and Money

Clare Boothe began a brief stint working for the Women's National party in 1921. She signed on as Alva Belmont's assistant and visited several cities on behalf of the new organization. She attended meetings, answered correspondence, and arranged interviews. On one occasion she even dropped leaflets from an open-cockpit plane as it flew over the city of Seneca Falls, New York. Belmont hoped that Boothe's intelligence, speaking ability, and charm would help popularize the women's rights movement. As predicted, her looks and charisma drew reporters and photographers who might otherwise have ignored a feminist speaker. Biographer Stephen Shadegg observed that "Clare's assignment was to attract public attention, enlist new converts, and help destroy the notion that feminine activists had to be rich, chesty old ma-

trons or disgruntled, plain spinsters—in short, to radiate youth and sex appeal."

Alva Belmont was not the only one banking on Boothe's sex appeal. Ann Austin hatched a ridiculous scheme after she learned that the heir to the throne of Great Britain, Edward, prince of Wales, was staying at a Virginia hotel. The hotel's manager was a friend of hers, and Austin persuaded him to arrange a ball in Edward's honor. Her hope was that the prince would be instantly captivated by her daughter, just as if he and Clare Boothe were characters in the movies.

But Austin's plan developed into a comedy of errors, not a Hollywood-style romance. Boothe and her mother arrived at the hotel in time for the ball, but their luggage did not. With no gown to wear, Boothe had to sit out

Alva Ertskin Belmont (center), the founder of the Women's National party, meets with supporters. Boothe worked for the feminist political group in 1921.

the ball, and she never met Prince Edward.

Although she had lost her chance to marry a prince, Boothe would soon find the next-best thing—or so it seemed at the time. George Tuttle Brokaw, a 43-year-old bachelor, was the distinguished-looking heir to a large fortune. Introduced to Boothe by mutual friends, he was so taken with her

that he called her home the very next day to ask Mrs. Austin for permission to begin seeing her daughter socially. Needless to say, Ann Austin needed very little convincing.

Having secured her mother's permission, Brokaw began to pursue Boothe in earnest. He called on her in his gleaming yellow motorcar, escorted her around town, gave her gifts, and finally brought her to his Fifth Avenue mansion to meet his 86-year-old mother. After Mrs. Brokaw gave Boothe the nod, George Brokaw presented her with a 17-carat diamond-solitaire engagement ring. Then he called on the Austins to discuss plans for the marriage.

Twenty-year-old Clare Boothe felt curiously left out of the proceedings, as if she were a child forced to sit idly by while the "grown-ups" decided her fate. Her future husband was 23 years older than she, a playboy with a reputation for courting and discarding women, and a member of a society family that considered Boothe a fortune hunter. But these facts were disregarded. Clare Luce later told Wilfrid Sheed that her first marriage was "arranged practically behind her back, like a baseball trade."

On August 10, 1923, Boothe and George Brokaw were married. One society reporter described the festivities as "the most important social event of the season." Following a glittering ceremony and a reception with 2,500 invited guests, the couple left on an extravagant, four-month honeymoon in Europe.

Clare Boothe was now Clare Boothe Brokaw, and she did her skillful best to live up to the demands of that name. She gave parties and balls, appeared at all the "right" social events, and allowed herself to be photographed and interviewed by gossip columnists and society reporters. But despite all her efforts and the support of her husband and mother-in-law, she was never accepted by the rest of his family. Luce later told a biographer that she heard the word *prostitute* whispered in reference to her at family gatherings.

The new Mrs. Brokaw tried valiantly to gain acceptance on another front— among the old-money society that spent summers in luxurious Newport, Rhode Island. She attempted to use her wit to impress the men and women her husband introduced her to, but she soon found that birth was more important than personality or accomplishment in Brokaw's circle of friends. For his biography of Luce, Sheed interviewed a Newport resident who reported that Clare Brokaw's parties were often shunned by the society "swells" on her guest list. According to Sheed, this woman remembered being "very touched by young Clare, sitting brave and alone at these and other gatherings and being snubbed by the world's finest."

Clare Boothe married George Brokaw on August 10, 1923. The lavish ceremony and reception were described in gossip columns across the country.

Even in face of these obstacles, the marriage seemed to be a happy one. Clare Brokaw was appreciative when her husband set her brother David up in the stock market, where he soon learned to make an easy living. George Brokaw was clearly in love with his young wife, and the future looked even

Clare and George Brokaw enjoy a summer outing. Initially happy, their marriage deteriorated as George Brokaw succumbed to alcoholism.

brighter when she became pregnant. The couple was overjoyed at the birth of their daughter, whom they named Ann, on August 24, 1924.

However, the Brokaws' marriage slowly deteriorated. George Brokaw had been a heavy drinker before his marriage, and he soon resumed his old habits. Although he was a quiet and charming man when sober, his wife later reported that during his drinking bouts he was "an ugly, murderously violent drunk" who was occasionally followed around by a servant carrying a straitjacket to prevent him from becoming a threat to himself or others. Unfortunately, Clare Brokaw sometimes had to face her husband alone. Probably because of his physical abuse, she suffered four miscarriages during their marriage. As Brokaw's behavior worsened, his wife slipped into despair and even began to entertain violent fantasies. She later told writer Dominick Dunne: "Once, I can remember coming home from a party and walking up our vast marble staircase at the Fifth Avenue house while he was striking me. I thought, if I just gave him one shove down the staircase I would be rid of him forever."

A desperate Clare Brokaw finally decided to sue for divorce after six years of marriage. As many women did at that time, she and her daughter briefly moved to Reno, Nevada, to take advantage of that state's liberal divorce laws. The final settlement awarded her a

Clare Boothe Brokaw embraces her only child, Ann. After six years of marriage, she divorced Ann's father in 1929.

trust fund of $425,000 and $26,000 a year for living expenses—a very generous figure at a time when a new Chevrolet sedan sold for $600. Clare Boothe (she often used her maiden name after the divorce) was now financially secure, but considering George Brokaw's fortune, the settlement was a modest one. Given her husband's brutality and drinking problem, she could have gotten much more money, but she was after financial security, not wealth. "I may have married for money," she later quipped, "but I certainly didn't divorce for it."

As 1929 drew to a close, Boothe was

Clare Brokaw (right) and an elegant friend chat outside a Fifth Avenue hotel. "We had so much of what we wanted," she wrote of this period. "Why weren't we happy?"

an attractive 26-year-old divorcée living with her daughter and four servants in an elegant, glass-and-chrome penthouse apartment in Manhattan. This luxurious life-style might have delighted many people, but it left Boothe feeling bored and useless. She began psychoanalysis but stopped when she decided that "analysis is the disease for which it pretends to be the cure." She had a fairly busy social life but found many of her acquaintances shallow and uninteresting. Years later, she wrote about the life she and her friends led during this period: "The New York of my youth was a fat, rich, glittering, exciting, glamorous place. We wanted so much of what we had, and we had so much of what we wanted. Why weren't we happy?"

Finally, she decided that her life needed a drastic change that she alone could effect. Although women who pursued careers were rarities at that time, she felt that employment might be her only escape from a life that revolved around parties, gossip, and fashion. Boothe needed courage and ingenuity to begin a career. Her friend Wilfrid Sheed observed that "back in 1929, Clare had no career models, no counselors worth a damn, nothing but her own mother wit. She simply had to invent herself, for better or worse."

With her background and interests, the best job for Clare Boothe would involve writing. One of her social acquaintances was magazine publisher

Condé Nast, an elegant man-about-town. Fortuitously seated next to him at a dinner party one evening, she asked him for a job on one of his publications, the fashion magazine *Vogue*. His response, as she later told Stephen Shadegg, was brusque. "My dear girl," he said, "I've had many like you come and ask for jobs but you won't stick it out." He told her that he was leaving for Europe the next day but that she could leave her name with *Vogue*'s editor, Edna Woolman Chase.

The first time Boothe dropped in at the magazine's offices Chase rebuffed her, but on her second visit she found that the editor had joined her boss in Europe. She noticed a few empty desks and was told that their occupants had recently quit. Boothe simply sat down at one of the vacant desks and announced that she was ready to go to work.

Apparently organization was a little lax at *Vogue*, because she was taken at her word and given the task of writing captions for fashion photographs. "The girl came around with pay envelopes at the end of the week," Clare Boothe Luce reported later, "and she was puzzled that there was no envelope with my name on it. I explained that Mr. Nast and Mrs. Chase were in Europe, and that I hoped they would straighten out my salary when they returned."

Three weeks later Nast returned from Europe to find that his new cap-

Miguel Covarrubias caricatured Clare Boothe Brokaw at the height of her Vanity Fair *career. Beginning as an assistant in 1930, she quickly rose to managing editor.*

tion writer had done brilliantly. Recognizing her talents—and realizing that he had underestimated her serious interest in pursuing a magazine career—he hired her at the respectable salary of $35 a week. Soon afterward she set her sights on another Nast publication, *Vanity Fair*, a magazine devoted to style, satire, and the best in contemporary fiction. Through her acquaintance with Donald Freeman, its

Clare Brokaw suns with her daughter in South Hampton, Long Island, in 1929—the year she dissolved her first marriage and embarked on a career in publishing.

managing editor, she earned a tryout. After proving her value, she transferred to *Vanity Fair* as an assistant editor.

Boothe learned her trade from the bottom up. She took notes for photographers, proofread, helped with page layouts, and edited the writing of others. Although her French was a bit rusty, she insisted that she was fluent in the language in order to impress her superiors. Armed with a French-English dictionary, she translated the

works of such distinguished authors as André Maurois and Paul Morand.

As they would throughout her lifetime, Boothe's boldness and diligence paid off. She won a promotion and began selecting pieces for the magazine. Finally she submitted one of her own essays, a deft satire on social chitchat, under the name of Julian Jerome. Managing editor Donald Freeman was impressed by the piece. "This fellow Julian Jerome has got some-

Impoverished New Yorkers line up to buy inexpensive milk during the Great Depression. Clare Boothe began her career during this period, when millions were without jobs.

thing," he told Boothe. "Find out who he is and get him down here." Boothe happily confessed that Jerome was already in the *Vanity Fair* offices. "Talking Up—and Thinking Down" became her first published work when it appeared—under her pen name—in August 1930.

The August issue also introduced one of her feature ideas, a companion to the magazine's popular "We Nominate for the Hall of Fame" section. This new feature, dubbed "We Nominate for Oblivion," consisted of a drawing that caricatured a prominent person accompanied by a caption explaining briefly and very frankly why that individual had outstayed his or her welcome in society. For example, Iowa senator Smith W. Brookhart was blasted as "one of the most triumphantly little provincial bores in the U.S. Congress." As Wilfrid Sheed pointed out, each of Boothe's breezy yet barbed pieces was "not a report but a performance," and each depended "entirely on flourishes of wit and style." Clare Boothe was well endowed with both.

Her writing career began to take off during this period. She turned out a stream of essays on the follies of America's social elite. With titles such as "Life Among the Snobs," many of these humorous pieces concerned the rivalry between a pair of stuffy society women she named Mrs. Topping and Mrs. Towerly. On the advice of the political columnist Arthur Krock, in 1931 she selected the best and sharpest of these essays and had them published as a book entitled *Stuffed Shirts*. Biographer Wilfrid Sheed has theorized that these satirical pieces represented Boothe's revenge on the men and women who snubbed her during her marriage to George Brokaw. He also points out that she was striking back at "high society" in general, "the magic mountain women like her had to climb if they wanted to climb at all in the twenties: a mountain composed of diamonds and quicksand."

Boothe's writing began to take on a slightly more serious tone as the effects of economic decline were felt across the country, even in the editorial offices of glossy magazines such as *Vanity Fair*. The stock market had crashed in 1929, touching off the Great Depression. At the height of the depression, 12 million people were unemployed, and even many of those who were able to find work faced daily hardship.

Regardless of their political orientation, many Americans were unhappy with Herbert Hoover, the Republican president who appeared to be doing nothing to help the country recover. Yet it seemed that the Democratic party was unable to offer an attractive alternative to Hoover and his hands-off approach to the economy. Condé Nast encouraged some of his writers to publicize the idea of an alternative political party, called the New National party. Boothe was asked to serve as the organization's executive secretary. Although the party never got off the ground, a phrase that would soon be on the lips of millions of Americans appeared in a pamphlet issued by the group. The slogan, which may have been Boothe's idea, was "A New Deal for America." A Democrat named Franklin Delano Roosevelt would soon rise to prominence with his own "New Deal," the official name of a whole package of reforms he would introduce as president.

Boothe's work with the short-lived New National party had given her a taste for the excitement of national politics. She was also polishing her skills and gaining a solid reputation at *Vanity Fair*, where she was now responsible for a number of its regular features.

One of her responsibilities at the

magazine was an immensely popular feature called "The Impossible Interview." This section featured a fictitious conversation, often written by Boothe, between two well-known but totally unlike public figures. The personalities of the subjects were exaggerated for effect, but the real humor came from the imagined interaction between the two participants. In a feature that paired American industrialist John D. Rockefeller with Soviet leader Joseph Stalin, for example, Rockefeller asks about Stalin's Five-Year Plan for economic growth. "Do you run this plan?" Rockefeller inquires, and Stalin nods. Rockefeller then asks, "Can the people still take it?" The ironfisted dictator's answer is simple and to the point: "Take it from me, they take it."

When Donald Freeman was killed in a car accident, Nast moved Boothe into his position as *Vanity Fair*'s managing editor. She was introduced to the magazine's readers in glowing terms: "An able editor, she speaks four languages, likes Backgammon, swimming, Persian

A popular Vanity Fair *feature was "The Impossible Interview." Here, dictators Stalin, Mussolini, and Hitler meet with American politician Huey Long.*

cats, collecting first editions, Ping-Pong, and Proust." Clare Boothe had worked her way up from minor assistant to managing editor in less than two years. But her career was far from over.

Thirty-year-old Clare Boothe projects a professional image in this 1933 portrait. She had become the managing editor of Vanity Fair *the previous year.*

FOUR

Coming of Age

The clamor of political debate filled the air in the summer of 1932. Clare Boothe plunged into the fray when her boss, Condé Nast, assigned her to cover the Democratic party convention in Chicago. The convention opened at a critical time in American history. The Great Depression had grown steadily worse; unemployment was increasing, and businesses and banks were failing. The Republican administration under Hoover clearly had no program to cope with the looming crisis. On the Democratic side, however, a clear alternative had emerged in the person of New York governor Franklin D. Roosevelt.

Boothe was there when Roosevelt officially became his party's presidential candidate on July 1, 1932. Roosevelt's dramatic acceptance speech promised that every person who was hungry would be fed and given a job.

He outlined an entire package of reforms to turn the economy around. "I pledge you, I pledge myself," he said as he concluded his stirring speech, "to a new deal for the American people." Along with the other staff members of *Vanity Fair*, Boothe swung her support behind Roosevelt.

She began to seek out and talk to important Democratic party supporters, including wealthy businessman Bernard Baruch. Although he never held an elective office, Baruch was an important adviser to Washington's highest officials. He would soon become a significant influence on Boothe's life and career, serving as her trusted counselor and intimate friend until his death in 1965.

Roosevelt was elected president by a landslide in the 1932 election, and his administration rushed like a tornado

A 1933 Vanity Fair *caricature dubbed Boothe's friend and political adviser Bernard Baruch "Wall Street's Gift to Government."*

bright and imaginative young people and brought them to Washington. Their ideas were then funneled up to what Roosevelt called his Brain Trust, a small group of senior advisers who made the final decisions on which proposals would become programs affecting the whole country.

Boothe may have had an important effect on these programs. Dining one evening with General Hugh Johnson, a member of the Brain Trust, she suggested that he look into the success of Italy's new economic controls. Instituted by Benito Mussolini's Fascist party, the system seemed to have turned around the country's flagging economy. Committees, called authorities, had been set up for nearly every Italian industry. Each authority determined the economic conditions for its particular industry, including wages, prices, and working hours.

General Johnson passed the idea on up, where it was received with favor and finally landed on the president's desk. When Roosevelt approved the idea, an American version of the Italian plan was put into effect under the title of National Recovery Administration (NRA). Johnson, who oversaw the operation, appointed Boothe to the Motion Picture Authority.

Boothe's first taste of government administration was a valuable learning experience, but she soon came to see the NRA as a first step toward widespread government interference with the free-

through the sleepy town of Washington, D.C. Before Roosevelt took office, the federal government had been relatively limited in scope, with a small number of employees and few programs that affected the whole country. Herbert Hoover, the president who preceded Roosevelt, was the first occupant of the White House even to have a phone on his desk or to employ more than one secretary. Within months of Roosevelt's inauguration, however, the number of federal employees and agencies had multiplied more than tenfold. The president sought out

Women harvest hops in a job created by Roosevelt's National Recovery Administration (NRA). Boothe originally proposed the idea for the NRA, but later withdrew her support.

dom of the marketplace. She was uncomfortable that businesses were forced to comply with NRA dictates and increasingly uneasy with the plan's origins in Mussolini's brutal dictatorship. Within a few months, Boothe resigned her position and returned to full-time work at *Vanity Fair*.

Her chief memory of that first plunge into national politics was her impression of Roosevelt himself. He overwhelmed her with his cleverness and ability but put her off with his sexist tendency to treat women like children. Her personal dislike of Roosevelt may have played a part in her later turn away from the Democratic party and its programs. Her relationship with the president would deteriorate further during the next several years.

Under Boothe's leadership, *Vanity Fair* became more politically oriented than it had been in the past—and more critical of Roosevelt and his programs. The president and his wife, formerly immune to personal attack in the magazine's pages, were caricatured in drawings and text, and Boothe penned some of the most stinging attacks herself. In a 1933 article, she eloquently expressed her skepticism about Roosevelt's New Deal by comparing the plan to a Hollywood film extravaganza: "Authored by an aspiring and heretofore unknown group of politico-economists hopefully dubbed the Brain Trust, produced by that gallant and daring *entrepreneur*, our current Pres-

ident, stage-managed by Congress—this 10-20-30 billion dollar thriller promises the public—poor compelled audience—a conventional Happy Ending of the depression."

Boothe did more than just write some of *Vanity Fair*'s best articles; she also came up with scores of innovative story ideas, oversaw the magazine's talented staff, and emerged as a gifted editor. Veteran editor Frank Crowninshield later said of Boothe that "during a stretch of fifty troubled years of editing, I have never encountered a Managing Editor so able, so daring, or so resourceful." Another compliment Boothe received reflected the era's ambivalent attitude about working women. One of her co-workers admiringly described Boothe as "a female who had male ideas."

But despite the best efforts of Boothe and her staff, the Great Depression was taking its toll on *Vanity Fair*'s circulation. In an attempt to halt this trend, publisher Condé Nast considered drastically changing the magazine. He asked his staff to come up with ideas for a completely new kind of publication. Boothe's suggestion, worked out in collaboration with her art department, was for a combination of text and candid photographs; the publication's name would come from a humor magazine that had recently gone bankrupt. She entitled the proposal "Changing Vanity Fair into a picture magazine called 'Life.'" When Nast de-

Franklin Delano Roosevelt (in car) visits an impoverished rural area in 1935. Roosevelt redefined and enlarged the government's role during his four terms as president.

Boothe cuts a fashionable figure for Vogue *magazine. She poked fun at "high society" in her 1933 collection of satirical essays,* Stuffed Shirts.

cided to stick with the magazine's present format, she filed her proposal away.

In late 1933 Boothe took a break from her writing and editing duties to vacation in Europe. Her position as managing editor of *Vanity Fair*, which published the work of leading writers in America and Europe, gave her access to literary circles in London, Paris, and Rome. While she was in England her friend Bernard Baruch introduced her to Winston Churchill, who would

later become Boothe's close friend—and Great Britain's prime minister. At that first meeting with Churchill, she drew on her almost uncanny ability to remain unruffled in the presence of dignitaries. This trait enabled her to earn their confidence and dispense with the formalities observed by the awestricken. "Clare," Wilfrid Sheed wrote, "with her amused voice, reduced the Great World to room-size instead."

When Boothe returned to the United States, she resigned from *Vanity Fair* in order to devote her time and energies completely to what she described to her friends as "serious journalism." She signed on with publisher William Randolph Hearst's newspaper chain to write a weekly column from Europe and returned to the Continent, where she interviewed political leaders as well as ordinary citizens. These encounters convinced her that dictators such as Italy's Mussolini and Germany's Adolf Hitler were silencing the citizenry and creating an unhealthy atmosphere of fear that permeated their respective countries. Many of her columns were frank expressions of her conclusions.

Unfortunately, she was soon embroiled in serious disagreements with her editor, Paul Block. One source of friction was Block's attempt to steer Boothe away from politics and restrict her writing to reports of society events. Even more serious disagreements arose over the content of her political articles. A conflict as old as the American republic had resurfaced, and Boothe and the Hearst organization were on opposite sides. Hearst was an "isolationist," one who believed that America should maintain as little economic and political contact as possible with the rest of the world. Although Boothe had begun her work with no strong convictions about international affairs, her encounters in Europe were rapidly turning her into an "interventionist," one who thought that the United States had legitimate international interests and should exercise its influence around the world. Her reports eloquently reflected her views. As a result, very few of her columns were printed, and she was eventually fired.

Boothe returned to New York, began work on a play, and plunged back into Manhattan's social whirl. One fateful evening she attended a gala party for songwriter Cole Porter at the posh Waldorf-Astoria Hotel. As she sat at a table on the edge of the ballroom, listening to musical-comedy star Ethel Merman singing Porter's songs, she noticed a familiar-looking man carrying two glasses of champagne. He was Henry R. Luce, known to his friends as Harry. Luce was the founder, publisher, and owner of *Time* and *Fortune* magazines. Boothe had met him once or twice before, and when he paused near her table she asked, "Is that champagne for me?"

Boothe attends a gathering with British prime minister Winston Churchill (right). Their longtime friendship centered around a love of politics and painting.

According to biographer Stephen Shadegg's account of this pivotal meeting, Luce joined Boothe for a long, wide-ranging conversation. He could be overbearing, even rude, but he was also an intense and fascinating conversationalist. When the party was over they were still talking. As they walked down to the empty lobby of the hotel to say good-bye, Luce told her, quite unexpectedly, that she was the kind of woman he had been looking for and that he planned to marry her.

Luce told Boothe that he would call on her in three days at precisely 3:30 in the afternoon but would have to leave at 4:00. He kept his word and showed

Clare Boothe and magazine publisher Henry R. Luce make a striking couple as they leave a Broadway premiere in October 1935, a month before their wedding.

up at the meeting, where he presented a businesslike proposition: The two of them would spend a year getting to know one another, and if she then felt toward him the way he already felt about her, he would divorce his wife and they would be married. Then he checked his watch and left.

Boothe was intrigued by Luce's bizarre idea of courtship, but she decided to take a wait-and-see approach to his strange proposal. She continued working on her play and took a trip to Europe with a friend. Three weeks after they had arrived in France, Luce called her to say he was in Paris. From this point on, wherever Boothe traveled, whether to Italy or the Caribbean Islands, Luce would show up within a week or so, call her, and arrange to spend time with her. She later said that as she spent time with Luce, her initial mystification gave way to interest and finally to love.

Meanwhile Boothe completed her play, entitled *Abide with Me*. It opened on Broadway on November 21, 1935. The drama's plot, quite obviously based on some of her own marriage experiences, centered on a troubled family headed by a dominating older alcoholic and his young wife. At the play's end, a family member who has

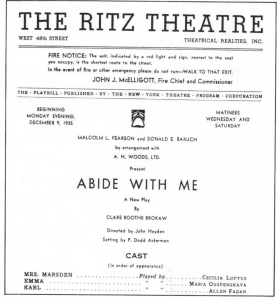

THE RITZ THEATRE

WEST 48th STREET   THEATRICAL REALTIES, INC.

FIRE NOTICE: The exit, indicated by a red light and sign, nearest to the seat you occupy, is the shortest route to the street.

In the event of fire or other emergency please do not run—WALK TO THAT EXIT.

JOHN J. McELLIGOTT, Fire Chief and Commissioner

THE · PLAYBILL · PUBLISHED · BY · THE · NEW · YORK · THEATRE · PROGRAM · CORPORATION

BEGINNING
MONDAY EVENING,
DECEMBER 9, 1935

MATINEES
WEDNESDAY AND
SATURDAY

MALCOLM L. PEARSON and DONALD E. BARUCH

by arrangement with

A. H. WOODS, LTD.

Present

ABIDE WITH ME

A New Play

By

CLARE BOOTHE BROKAW

Directed by John Hayden

Setting by P. Dodd Ackerman

CAST
(In order of appearance)

MRS. MARSDEN .... *Played by* .... CECILIA LOFTUS
EMMA .... " " ...... MARIA OUSPENSKAYA
KARL .... " " ...... ALLEN FAGAN

Abide with Me was Boothe's first produced play. The plot concerned an unhappy marriage similar to the playwright's union with George Brokaw.

been driven over the brink by the alcoholic's brutality finally shoots him. One critic called *Abide with Me* "too horrible to be real"; another chided the play's author for "sheer bad writing." The play closed after a month. But it seems likely that Boothe did not feel the production's failure too keenly, for she had other things on her mind. Two days after her play opened, she married Henry Luce in Greenwich, Connecticut.

According to writer Wilfrid Sheed, when Clare and Henry Luce were together "His gruffness sparkled, her flippancy was solemnified."

FIVE

Serious Comedy

After a brief honeymoon on a small yacht in the Caribbean, Clare and Henry Luce settled into comfortable and busy lives, shuttling between an apartment in New York and a house in Greenwich, Connecticut. Charismatic, attractive, and influential, they were a remarkable couple. Clare Luce was the witty, outgoing one; her husband the quiet, methodical thinker. As Sheed describes them, "The effect of them together was like an inspired clash of colors. It worked. His gruffness sparkled, her flippancy was solemnified."

Their house in Greenwich, and later the larger and more impressive estate that they bought in the nearby town of Ridgefield, became the setting for dinners that were described as "a social and intellectual banquet." Political leaders, artists, writers, and entertainment figures all made regular appearances at the Luces' parties. Many of their guests felt more at ease with their charming hostess than with their occasionally surly host. As Bernard Baruch recalled in his memoirs, "When Clare asks you a question, you know she will value your opinion, even though she disagrees with you. When Harry asks you a question, he might be setting you up to overwhelm you with his superior knowledge."

The Luce estate in Connecticut also provided a haven for the bride's family. Boothe had been concerned that Luce would not welcome the members of her family, but this fear turned out to be groundless. Henry Luce and her mother became good friends, and Ann Austin was a frequent visitor. Luce also befriended his wife's brother, David Boothe, and immediately contacted business associates to help Boothe get a job. And, most important to Clare Boothe Luce, her new husband got along exceptionally well with his stepdaughter, Ann, whom he referred to as "my daughter." Henry Luce was also helpful in settling Ann Brokaw's claims against the estate of her father, who had died in a sanatorium for alcoholics in May 1935.

Brilliant as their social life now was, however, it did not fill Clare Luce's time nor exhaust her energy. An experienced writer and editor, she hoped to acquire a spot on one of her husband's publications. But the all-male editorial staff of *Time* and *Fortune* objected to working with a woman— especially Clare Boothe Luce. They were concerned that as the publisher's wife, she might have more influence than any of them.

At this time Henry Luce and his senior editors were deeply involved in preliminary work on a new publication. Their plan called for a news magazine that used a mix of pictures and text to tell its stories, and they had decided to call it *Life*. A great deal has been written about Clare Luce's contribution to the idea, the name, and the founding of this magazine. Since neither she nor her husband ever revealed exactly what happened, there are several different accounts of the magazine's origins.

Similar publications already existed in France and England, and the name *Life* was one of the many that the Luce

Clare Boothe Luce's ideas were instrumental in the creation of her husband's publication Life, *but when she sought a job at the magazine, she was rebuffed.*

staff had considered, along with *Look*, *Scoop*, *Click*, and *Parade*. Therefore, Clare Luce could not claim that the idea and title for the new magazine were entirely hers. But the fact remains that she had pitched a remarkably similar magazine concept to Condé Nast years before her husband considered the idea. Nearly every account of the beginnings of *Life* magazine gives Clare Luce credit for bringing the general idea to her husband's attention and keeping him focused on it. After the magazine had published its first few issues, some members of Henry Luce's staff sued him on the grounds that he had stolen the idea for *Life* from them. At this point Clare Luce was able to bring out the copy of her proposal to Nast, which her husband used as evidence that the original ideas had been hers. The case was dismissed.

The first issue of *Life* appeared on November 19, 1936. Its immediate success was unexpected—so unexpected that it almost bankrupted the Luce publishing empire. Advertising rates for the new publication had been set too low, on the expectation that *Life* would sell no more than 250,000 copies a week. When the weekly demand for the magazine passed a million copies, production costs far exceeded the income from advertising. It was only a year later, after Henry Luce had invested $5 million of his own money, that advertising rates could be renegotiated and *Life* could begin to turn a profit.

As one of the prime forces behind the formation of the magazine, Clare Boothe Luce had expected to win a spot on *Life*'s staff. But her husband, perhaps bowing to pressure from his staff, refused to consider hiring her. Frustrated in all her attempts to get a job as an editor or staff correspondent on one of Henry Luce's publications, she returned to playwriting.

Luce later said that the idea for her

Luce displays a pheasant bagged during a hunting expedition. An avid sportswoman, she also enjoyed swimming and horseback riding.

new play, which she called *The Women*, came from a conversation she overheard in the powder room of a nightclub. The script called for an exceptionally large cast of 44 women and, to everyone's surprise, no men. The plot revolved around Mary Haines, a happily married woman who falls

55

Henry and Clare Luce (left and second from right) join friends at a posh night spot. A conversation overheard in a nightclub ladies' room inspired The Women.

prey to the schemes of her friends. Haines's circle of acquaintances, most of whom are idle, bored gossips, discover that her husband is having an affair with a glamorous young social climber named Crystal Allen. To amuse themselves, they arrange to have Haines discover the truth. A devastated Haines divorces her husband, who then marries Allen.

The rest of the play concerns the infidelities, divorces, and remarriages of Haines's friends over the next two years. Haines, who has learned something about plotting from her devious acquaintances, learns that Allen is having an affair with an actor. She cleverly arranges for her ex-husband to find out about his new wife's relationship and finally wins him back. Mary Haines's curtain line sums up her cynical conclusion that ruthlessness is required for survival in wealthy society: "I've had two years to sharpen my claws."

A number of the producers Luce approached for *The Women* turned it down, but an old friend, Max Gordon, finally agreed to produce it—on the condition that Luce make extensive changes in her script. To his surprise, she did so while rehearsals proceeded, often rewriting a whole scene in one evening.

The play had a number of weaknesses, in particular the repeated device of having a number of persons coincidentally arrive at the same place so that confrontation is inevitable. One also wonders why Haines, portrayed as a decent woman with high standards, does not simply find a new circle of friends. But overshadowing these faults are the play's many strengths, which help to explain why it became a smash success.

Perhaps foremost among these strengths was the playwright's famous wit, honed during her years at *Vanity Fair*. The dialogue sparkles, and many lines from *The Women* became the talk of New York theater circles. Among them are the boast by villainess Sylvia Fowler that "where I spit no grass grows ever" and the complaint by one character who hates watercress: "I'd rather eat my way across a front lawn." One woman describes another's lacquered red fingernails as looking as if she had "been tearing at somebody's throat."

Equally important was Luce's ability to handle a large cast of characters without blurring each one's sharply drawn identity. In addition, scenes that in more conventional plays would have been treated sentimentally were presented with an original twist and remarkably honest and straightforward dialogue. A touching scene between Haines and her pre-teen daughter evolves into a discussion of the girl's anxiety about changes taking place in her body. These two characters go on to talk about the restrictions faced by women in the job market. While acknowledging these prejudices, Haines firmly assures her daughter that women can do anything that men can do, a courageous statement in 1936. "These days," she tells her, "ladies do all the things men do. They fly aeroplanes across the ocean, they go into politics and business."

In spite of its frank portrayal of a side of women's lives that up to then had never been shown in public, *The Women* remained conservative in its conclusions about men, women, and their relationships. One of Luce's characters, presented as sensible and rather wise, characterizes men as "just animals" and goes on to ask, "Who are we to quarrel with the way God made them?" Most of the women in the play are opportunistic, scheming, and selfish. Perhaps the most pessimistic aspect of Luce's play is its failure to challenge the traditional notion that women will do whatever it takes to "catch" a man, even if this involves overlooking male infidelity or viciously competing with female friends. Near

Actress Rosalind Russell (in hat) is restrained by costar Norma Shearer in this scene from the 1949 movie version of Luce's The Women.

the end of the play, Mary Haines utters the playwright's grim conclusion that "Pride is a luxury that a woman in love can't afford."

Especially in recent years, critics have attacked the play's cynical conclusions about sex roles, but it is possible that Luce, a lifelong feminist, exaggerated her characters' personalities to draw attention to the distortions caused by sex stereotyping. Luce may have had her characters bitterly wage war against each other in order to criticize cultural norms that made marriage to a successful man one of the few ways a woman could provide for herself and her children. Also, like her book *Stuffed Shirts*, *The Women* lampoons shallow, arrogant members of the upper class. Luce's play was an attack on a social reality, not women in general.

The Women opened on December 26, 1936, and immediately became the smash hit of the season, even of the decade. It ran for 657 performances on

Broadway and was twice made into a movie and once into a television play. It has been performed all over the world, in dozens of countries and languages, and is still being staged. Soldiers dressed as women even performed the play during World War II. Stephen Shadegg estimates that *The Women* earned its author more than $2 million.

The play marked an important turning point in Luce's life and career. Its success established her reputation as a leading playwright. It also meant an important step forward in her development as an individual. This was her first work as a writer in which her earnest intentions were given equal weight with her wit. Although on the surface *The Women* was a comedy, she meant it (and her audience certainly enjoyed it) as a "serious comedy"—one that contained important observations about human nature.

Luce's next hit play, *Kiss the Boys Goodbye*, also fused humor and morality. The play, which opened in September 1938, seemed to be a satire of the much-publicized search for an actress to play the coveted role of Scarlett O'Hara in *Gone with the Wind*. Luce had been in Hollywood working on a film version of *The Women* during the search for the perfect Scarlett and had witnessed the frenzied quest firsthand. Her brilliant light comedy poked fun at Hollywood's values, focusing on the greed, deceit, and clandestine romances that seemed at times to propel

the movie industry. In addition, Luce used humor to unmask the racist views of upper-class Americans, particularly those who claimed to be liberal. The play even demonstrated Luce's ability to laugh at herself. She and her husband had just bought an elegant South Carolina plantation known as Mepkin, and *Kiss the Boys Goodbye* features a crass publishing magnate and his wife who are frantically trying to adapt to life in the South, much to the amusement of their skeptical neighbors.

But in her introduction to the printed version of the play, published three months after its Broadway opening, Luce announced that her true purpose in writing *Kiss the Boys Goodbye* had been much more serious than anyone guessed. "This play," she wrote, "was meant to be a political allegory [a symbolic treatment] about Fascism in America. But everywhere it has been taken for a parody of Hollywood's search for Scarlett O'Hara." The rest of her introduction was an impassioned essay about fascism, the form of political dictatorship practiced by Italian leader Benito Mussolini and Germany's Adolf Hitler. According to Luce, "Southernism"—a way of life in the American South built on the oppression of blacks—was "a particular and highly matured form of Fascism with which America had lived more or less peacefully for seventy-five years." Southern belle Cindy Lou Bethany, the play's central character, was meant as

The Women *established Luce's reputation as a playwright. The witty comedy was a long-running hit on Broadway and is still staged today.*

"an American version of a Brown Shirt street brawler from Munich"—that is, one of Hitler's Nazi thugs.

Convinced that comedy obscured her heartfelt observations, Luce changed the tone of her writing. Her next play, *Margin for Error*, had light moments, but the drama delivered a clear political message. It presented an all-out attack on the Nazis' racist philosophy, expressed through the conflict between a Nazi diplomat and an American Jewish police officer assigned to guard the German consulate. *Margin for Error* opened on November 3, 1939. Like Luce's past two plays, it received a mixed response from the critics, but unlike its predecessors it was only moderately successful with the public.

Clare Luce's mother had been killed in an automobile accident the year before *Margin for Error* was produced. The death of her lighthearted, loving mother was a sobering loss for Luce. Wilfrid Sheed theorized that "the theatrical, champagne-out-of-a-shoe side of Clare may have died with her, or at least grown paler." Certainly *Margin for Error* reflected a new side of Clare Boothe Luce: the serious commentator on international politics.

Concerned that the countries of Europe were sliding toward war, Luce decided to travel to the Continent in order to observe political developments firsthand. Part of the inspiration for her trip was a recent poll in which

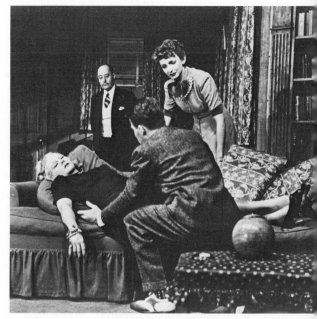

Audiences and critics saw Kiss the Boys Goodbye *as a comedy about Hollywood, but Luce intended it as political satire.*

two-thirds of Americans predicted that the country would never again participate in a European war and more than 70 percent said that they did not think the United States should get involved even if the nation's longtime ally, England, was invaded by Germany. Luce's last stint in Europe had convinced her that these isolationist views were potentially dangerous, and she "just had to find out whether this war is our business or not." She could only get State Department permission for the trip if she went as a journalist. In this roundabout way she finally won a job in Henry Luce's publishing empire, as a roving correspondent for

In her 1939 drama Margin for Error, *Luce sought to convey her political convictions. Unlike her past two efforts, the play was not very popular.*

Life. She sailed for Italy on February 24, 1940.

The German army had by this time occupied Austria and Poland, and war was certainly in the air, but the Italians Luce met seemed unconcerned. Discouraged, she moved on to Paris, where the prevailing opinion seemed to be that there would most certainly be a European war, that it would be a long war, but that of course Germany would lose again. France, her sources assured her, was in no danger at all, because it was protected by the Maginot Line.

The Maginot Line was an extensive system of fortified defenses stretching across France's eastern border. Its cost had nearly bankrupted the government, but most of the population thought that the Maginot Line was well worth the expense. It was, the French believed, "unthinkable" that Hitler's troops could crack such a defense. And so, Luce wrote, "France, in the spring, marked time, and talked and talked and talked."

Luce had been named "godmother" of one of the forts in the Maginot system, and she used this connection to become the first woman to visit the line. She found miles of countryside where fields "were punctured by the ugly protruding snouts of field guns." Hundreds of cement pillboxes were buried in the hills, steel spikes were embedded in the earth to repel tanks, and hundreds of thousands of well-armed French soldiers stood ready, hidden in the woods. All these bristling defenses were aimed at a silent German army, entrenched only a few miles to the east.

The line was punctuated at regular intervals with underground "cities" called forts, each able to sustain thousands of defenders behind impregnable barriers. As far as Luce could see, the line of defenses could not be overcome by direct assault, even by Hitler's famed armored divisions. She should have felt reassured, but she was not. "I was just beginning to suspect," she wrote, "that France and England had been dangerously lulled to sleep by the dangerous illusion that they had both time and impregnable defenses." America, she thought, was making the same mistake; its Maginot Line was the Atlantic Ocean.

She moved on to England, where she was dismayed by "the smugness and complacency of the British." In the Netherlands, a few days later, the prevailing attitude was summed up by the secretary general for foreign affairs: "One does one's best, one waits, one accepts the inevitable." Then the Germans invaded Denmark, Norway, and Sweden, and it was clear that there

German troops march into a Belgian town in 1940. Although many Americans had been unconcerned, Luce had foreseen the European conflict that would escalate into World War II.

was no longer time to wait and watch. Luce cabled her husband, "Come, the curtain is going up."

Henry Luce joined his wife in the middle of April 1940, and the two of them stayed with the American ambassador in Brussels, Belgium. They were awakened at dawn one morning by a German air raid. According to Clare Luce's vivid description,

about twenty planes, very high up, came over in formation. Their bellies gleamed in the gold and red sunrise. Then I heard a thin long, long whistle and a terrible round *bam!* The whistle was from the bomb that pierced the roof of a three-storied house across the

63

French refugees flee Nazi invaders. When Hitler entered Belgium and France, the Luces left Belgium along with millions of others.

square, and the *bam* was the glut and vomit of glass and wood and stone that was hurled into the little green park before me.

The Germans advanced through Belgium and circled around the northern end of France's Maginot Line, bypassing it and settling the issue of its value as a defense. The line's mounted guns could not be moved to fire at the invading Germans because the artillery was fixed in concrete and could fire only toward the east.

By this time it was clear that the Luces were no longer safe in Europe. Together with a streaming horde of refugees who clogged the roads and rails, the couple hastened back to Paris. Henry Luce then left for America,

but his wife insisted on staying long enough to finish collecting the material for her book.

Clare Luce continued traveling across the Continent, venturing even to the front lines. She was astonished when the French censors prevented her from sending her reports back to the United States. All that Americans were able to read at this time was that Germany and France were negotiating a peaceful settlement. She angrily wrote that she and her journalist colleagues were "gagged by the violence of incredibly stupid French censorship [and] hamstrung by criminal American indifference to the real issues at stake." When someone advised her, "Wait till the war blows over," she answered

Italian Fascist leader Benito Mussolini exhorts his troops to prepare for war. Luce's Europe in the Spring *chronicled the events that led to World War II.*

bitterly, "Blows over what—the Atlantic?"

Luce returned to the United States and published *Europe in the Spring*, a book that quickly became a best-seller. Her introduction breezily described the work as "just a confused, hastily written eye- and ear-witness report, a sad sheaf of notes on a few sad cities inhabited by many sad, confused people." But the volume was more than that. *Europe in the Spring* dealt vigorously and passionately with what she called the "lethal inertia, woeful ignorance, blind patriotism, corroding jealousies, mortal miscalculation, and criminal complacency" of the people of Europe—especially their leaders— in the face of Hitler's threat to democ-

racy. Wilfrid Sheed later called the book "easily her best claim as a global thinker" but pointed out that the seriousness of her message was compromised by the publisher's decision to include "a preposterously glamorous picture of Clare on the jacket, no doubt a good selling point in 1940, but fatally undercutting the serious work within."

Europe in the Spring received a warm reception in the United States. Reprinted eight times, the book helped shape public opinion as Americans tried to make sense of the escalating crisis in Europe. But Clare Boothe Luce did not rest on her laurels. A new arena would soon beckon to the successful overseas correspondent and author: the world of American politics.

Clare Boothe Luce began a political career in 1942, but she continued writing. "I can't avoid writing," she joked. "It's a sort of nervous tic."

National Politics

Clare Luce had returned to the United States convinced that Hitler would very soon conquer France and invade England. In her eyes, the survival of democratic Europe depended on America. Yet despite Hitler's advances across the Continent, many Americans were still strongly isolationist. President Roosevelt, repeatedly stalling on requests for aid from his friend, Prime Minister Winston Churchill of England, seemed to Luce to be more interested in campaigning for a third term as president than in preparing the nation for an inevitable war.

The president's attitude was only one of the reasons that Luce had shifted to an anti-Roosevelt position. Her early disenchantment with the programs of the National Recovery Administration had led her to distrust all his domestic policies, and she felt that

he was much too tolerant of the dangers of communism. Nor did she like Roosevelt personally—and the feeling was mutual. At one White House function, Luce overheard the president tell an aide to "get that woman out of here." She also disliked Eleanor Roosevelt, the president's wife, but she respected the first lady's efforts on behalf of the poor, blacks, and women. With characteristic brevity, Luce said of Roosevelt: "No woman has ever so comforted the distressed, or so distressed the comfortable."

In the 1940 presidential campaign, Luce and her husband put their efforts behind the nomination and election of Republican Wendell Willkie, whom they supported for his interventionist foreign policy and conservative views on domestic issues. Clare Luce made her first public speech in October; by

Life correspondent Clare Boothe Luce is greeted by Chinese leader Chiang Kai-shek (left) and his wife during a 1941 visit to the Far East.

the campaign's end she had made more than 40 appearances at pro-Willkie rallies. However, Willkie did not wage a strong campaign and Roosevelt won his third term without difficulty.

At this time there was another war going on, one that barely engaged the attention of Americans—although that situation would soon change. Japan had invaded China and threatened to overrun the country. The son of missionaries, Henry Luce had been born in China and had a strong interest in that nation's fate. Although Clare Luce knew little of the Far East and was primarily interested in European af-

fairs, she accompanied her husband on a 1941 trip to Asia. They made a remarkably effective team of reporters for *Life* magazine. She was the keen observer and brilliant writer, he the intense and tireless investigator.

The Luces visited the front, where Chinese and Japanese troops were locked in a stalemate. Clare Luce wrote two articles about the explosive situation in Asia, drawing on her firsthand experiences on the front lines as well as interviews with influential leaders such as Indian prime minister Jawaharlal Nehru and China's leader, Chiang Kai-shek. She also reported on

Luce and her daughter, Ann Brokaw, enjoyed a warm relationship. Despite her busy career, Clare Luce usually found time for her only child.

the plight of the inhabitants of war-torn cities. Luce's vivid war stories would captivate her readers back home, but they would also draw criticism. Dorothy Parker, for example, felt that Luce emphasized herself too much in her articles and dubbed her war correspondence "All Clare on the Western Front."

Convinced that the Chinese could hold out if they received sufficient supplies from America and England, the Luces flew home, determined to drum up support for the Chinese government. In order to popularize her conviction that Americans must face

the inevitability of global conflict, Clare Luce began work on a biography of Homer Lea, an American general who 30 years before had predicted in detail the outbreak of war between Germany and England and between China and Japan. She spent the summer of 1941 working on the manuscript at her Connecticut home. For the first time in many years, she had an uninterrupted two months with her daughter Ann, who had just graduated with honors from Virginia's prestigious Foxcroft School.

At the end of the summer Ann went off to Stanford University in California.

Her book finished, Luce herself went on to the Philippines for another reportorial trip. There she found a startling, and depressing, similarity to the indifference she had seen in France and England more than a year earlier. Her major interview on this trip was with General Douglas MacArthur, who very soon was to inspire the war effort with his courageous leadership of the American resistance to invading Japanese forces. Luce admired MacArthur's leadership ability, but in a letter to the editor of *Life* she remarked that he was "so taken with himself as a prophet that he often spoke nonsense."

Luce's interview appeared with perfect timing as the cover story for *Life* on December 8, 1941, the day after the Japanese bombed the U.S. fleet docked in Pearl Harbor, Hawaii. The bombing killed more than 3,000 Americans, severely damaged the U.S. fleet, and brought the United States into war with Japan, Germany, and their allies.

A few of the contacts Luce had made during her visits to the Far East had assured her that the Japanese could not have launched an offensive without the U.S. government's knowledge. She believed that President Roosevelt had known about the bombing in advance but had allowed it to take place because a Japanese attack on American soil would enflame public opinion and garner support for the war. When Roosevelt ran for reelection in 1944, Luce would shock many Americans by charging that he "lied the American people into war because he could not lead them into it."

After Luce's 1942 trip to Burma—where she chronicled the Allies' unsuccessful attempt to hold off invading Japanese forces—her career as a foreign correspondent had to be put aside until it was again possible to travel in war zones. But her strong convictions about the Allied cause did not permit her to sit still and watch the war go by. She had an established reputation as a writer and speaker who could handle significant issues, and she had demonstrated her grasp of international politics in dozens of articles as well as in *Europe in the Spring*. Clare Boothe Luce—editor, playwright, and war correspondent—decided to embark on a career in politics.

Although her entrance into the political arena surprised many observers, Luce apparently considered the idea for years. As early as 1932, she and some *Vanity Fair* staffers were discussing some legislation that the Senate was considering when one of her coworkers joked, "Maybe *you* will end up in the Senate!" Failing to see the humor of this idea, she shot her subordinate a withering look and unsmilingly replied, "Stranger things could happen."

Once Luce made up her mind to seek public office, she plunged into the project with all her considerable energy. Despite the largely Democratic

70

Servicemen swarm down the side of a U.S. ship torpedoed by the Japanese during the December 7, 1941, attack on Pearl Harbor, Hawaii.

constituency of the Connecticut district she lived in, Luce—by this time a staunch Republican—decided to run for Congress in 1942. She ran an active and well-organized campaign for her party's nomination. She was the over- whelming favorite at the Republican convention, where she was nominated by a vote of 84 to 2. She then turned with equal energy and determination to the general election, which pitted her against newspaper publisher Le-

Congressional candidate Luce addresses a crowd in 1942. According to one journalist, she possessed "glow, intense conviction, and crusading zeal."

neutrality now that the owner's wife planned to run for public office. To play it safe, most of them chose to ignore her campaign. But that hardly mattered to Luce, who expected no special treatment.

She was waging an uphill battle. Besides being mostly Democratic, her congressional district was largely Catholic and working class. Luce, on the other hand, was Protestant and wealthy. Many voters in her district were immigrants' children who still felt strong ties to their ethnic backgrounds. Well aware of this fact, Luce appealed separately—and strongly—to each ethnic group. She met with Polish women, for example, to tell them she had been the last American woman out of Poland's capital, Warsaw, before the Nazis stormed the city. Luce ultimately won the election, but by the narrow margin of less than 7,000 ballots out of a total of 120,000 votes cast. She probably owed her victory to the votes of women eager to elect the first congresswoman from Connecticut.

In Washington, Clare Boothe Luce moved quickly into the spotlight. She impressed her colleagues with her ability to bolster her public pronouncements with an exceptional background in international affairs. In contrast to many of her fellow politicians, who were loyal to their political party at all costs, Luce immediately gained a reputation as an independent thinker. She seldom followed the party

roy Downs, the Democratic candidate. Luce campaigned tirelessly, crisscrossing her district to give speeches and seek out the public. An excellent speaker, Luce could talk convincingly on any point.

The staff of *Time* magazine, trying to report the news fairly, had some honest concerns about the magazine's

line or tried to skirt controversial issues, and she was usually quite blunt
when presenting her ideas. She was an
unusual congressional representative:
a wealthy Republican from a working-
class Democratic district, a newcomer
who knew more about foreign policy
than many of her peers, and a conservative who campaigned for blacks' civil
liberties and supported the rights of
labor and women.

As she attempted to carve out a
niche in public life, Luce occasionally
faltered. Although fledgling representatives were expected to refrain from
discussing political matters at the
president's traditional reception for
new members of Congress, she sent
Roosevelt a five-page list of issues that
she said she wanted to discuss at the
gathering. When he saw her there,
Roosevelt curtly dismissed her before
she could begin to make her case. He
shook her hand and asked "How's
Harry?" before turning away with a
wave of his cigarette holder. Her reputation as an aggressive upstart continued to grow as Luce lobbied for a seat
on the Foreign Relations Committee.
Unaware of Washington's complex et-
iquette, she did not know that this
group was traditionally made up of
senior members of the House. Her
request was denied, and her colleagues found a new reason to resent
her.

Luce also had to learn that the wit-
ticisms that had helped to establish

*Newly elected congresswoman Clare
Boothe Luce is surrounded by
photographers during her first
Washington press conference.*

her renown as a writer could be liabil-
ities to a congresswoman. She discovered this after she made her "maiden"
speech, the first prepared oration
given by a new representative. Luce
made her debut on February 9, 1943,
choosing "freedom of the skies" as her
theme. The debate over this issue revolved around each country's right to
regulate air traffic within its territory
once the war ended and commercial
air flights were resumed.

Representative Luce talks with First Lady Eleanor Roosevelt. Although the two women had their differences, they shared a commitment to social justice.

Luce's primary opponent on this issue was Vice-President Henry Wallace, a champion of the most liberal segments of the Democratic party. His view was that the skies, like the seas, should be open to any nation, without restriction. Luce, on the other hand, was concerned that foreign airlines would be able to undersell American operators, seriously damaging the still-young U.S. commercial airline industry. She summed up her position in these words:

Since the world began, there never was complete equality about anything. No nation will ever have the same number of planes, and flying hours in a year. Thus with appropriate patriotic feeling, I naturally want the United States of America to lead in the air. We should dominate the skies. In the Lord's infinite Heaven there is plenty of room for all nations. But our planes should fly in the greatest numbers, since I believe that we will be producing them in the greatest numbers.

The freshman representative's address might have passed unnoticed but for one word that Luce introduced into her attack on Wallace's position. It was the last word of a sentence that was picked up and repeated around the country: "Much of what Mr. Wallace calls his global thinking is, no matter how you slice it, still globaloney." Although she had delivered a carefully prepared presentation of her views on a significant international issue, much of what she said was forgotten in the newspaper publicity about her "globaloney speech." The media reaction to her maiden address was a sign of things to come: Throughout Luce's career in Congress, public accounts often distorted the actual text of her speeches.

The media kept Luce in the public eye, but to her chagrin she was treated more like a movie star than a legislator. Reporters concentrated on her personality, her more flamboyant public statements, and her private life. When one of her maids quit, for example, 17 different newspapers ran stories about the "event." Luce responded to the media circus with one of her typical quips: "Yes, we've lost an old family retainer who had been with us for almost two weeks."

Part of Luce's image problem was related to the era's stereotypes about women. Male celebrities were often valued for their ideas or achievements, female public figures for their looks or personalities. Women were often seen as over their heads in the political

Luce testifies on American-Chinese relations before the House Foreign Affairs Committee in 1943. Global policy claimed much of her attention as a congresswoman.

realm—and beautiful women were especially suspect. At one point another representative teased Luce about a poll that named her one of the six American women with the most beautiful legs. She responded that her brains, not her legs, had enabled her to succeed. "Don't you realize," she asked him, "that you are just falling for some subtle New Deal propaganda designed to distract attention from the end of me that is really functioning?"

Luce's reaction to these prejudices may have compounded her problem. In her previous roles as chic editor, witty

Luce prepares to address a Republican group. Her style and wit made her a popular speaker, but she was frustrated by the media's emphasis on her looks and personality.

playwright, or fashionable woman-about-town, Luce's demeanor was warm and sometimes slightly flirtatious. But in her new incarnation as stateswoman, she often turned off her charm in the interests of being taken seriously. Wilfrid Sheed observed that a woman "had to be very no-nonsense indeed (or else very plain-looking) to get a fair hearing in those days." Luce's carefully cultivated air of authority helped win the respect of some of her peers, but others considered her merely cold and domineering. One acquaintance even dubbed Clare Luce "a beautiful palace without central heating."

Because she was widely respected for her abilities as a public speaker, in September 1943 she was asked to tour through the Western states speaking to Republican groups. This program was planned as the first step in the party's effort to defeat Roosevelt when he ran, as he was expected to do, for a fourth term in 1944. She accepted willingly, for the tour would certainly help her become better known to Republican leaders. She had already told friends that she was seriously thinking of seeking higher office, first a Senate seat and then perhaps the vice-presidency. In addition, the trip would give her the chance to visit her daughter Ann, then in her junior year at Stanford.

On January 10, 1944, she flew to San Francisco where she had a fine visit with Ann, who only the day before had

Henry Luce attempts to shield his devastated wife from the press at Ann Brokaw's funeral. The 19-year-old was killed in a car accident in January 1944.

become engaged to a fellow student. Early the next morning, while Luce was still asleep, Ann and a friend drove back to Stanford, a half-hour's ride from the city. Those were the days before seatbelts. A car, driven recklessly by a Stanford teacher, shot out of a side street and plowed into the side of Ann's car.

Luce later recalled being awakened by her secretary: "'Wake up! Wake up! Your daughter's been killed. Ann is dead!' . . . She was shaking me by the shoulders, saying Ann had been thrown from the open car and hit a tree and broken her neck. It was so strange. . . . I called up Harry. I remember the first words he said: 'Not that beautiful girl.'" Author and journalist Marie Brenner called the death of Luce's 19-year-old daughter "the central tragedy of her life." Nothing would ever be the same for Clare Boothe Luce again.

Several months after her daughter's death, Clare Boothe Luce shook off her grief to campaign for Republican presidential nominee Thomas E. Dewey.

SEVEN

Change and Controversy

They buried Ann at Mepkin, the Luce estate in South Carolina. Clare Luce was devastated by the death of her only child and returned to Washington a sick woman, barely able to carry out her duties. "Her health is very poor," one of her friends remarked at the time; "I don't think she will survive."

Luce carried on in this subdued way for a few months, until she was asked to address the Republican national convention, which was convening that summer to name the party's candidates for president and vice-president. She began working with her old enthusiasm—but something had changed in Clare Luce. Her passion gave way to shrillness, her measured logic to wholly emotional appeals.

Luce's friends and biographers have asserted that the death of her daughter brought out the political street-brawler in Luce. According to Wilfrid Sheed, Ann's death drove her mother "into ever more flamboyant activity, and more bellicose politics." In his view, Luce's flamboyant behavior during the 1944 election campaign was "her response to grief; one must fight, one must live. Clare was often at her most outrageous when she was hurting all over." Author Marie Brenner agreed with this view, theorizing that Luce viciously lashed out at her political opponents "as she might have wished to lash out against the fates that had taken her daughter away from her."

The controversial speech she gave at the Republican convention was an all-out attack on President Roosevelt, who she alleged was responsible for the death of "G.I. Jim," her name for the soldiers who had died in World War II. As an interventionist, Luce herself was an ardent supporter of the war; her complaint against Roosevelt was that he had been reelected four years before by misleading the American people about the inevitability of the nation's involvement in the conflict. It was in this speech that she charged that Roosevelt had "lied the American people into war" by covering up his foreknowledge of the Japanese attack on Pearl Harbor. But by criticizing the president during a popular war, Luce was playing with fire.

Because of her unrelenting assault on Roosevelt, a beloved president whose name was synonymous with the Democratic party, the Democrats went all out to defeat her when she ran for reelection in 1944. Several of the "Celebrities for Roosevelt," a group that included writer Dorothy Parker, author and editor Clifton Fadiman, and playwright Edna Ferber, traveled to Luce's Connecticut district to denounce her. One of her critics, referring to her ancestor, Lincoln's assassin John Wilkes Booth, went so far as to say that "Representative Clare Boothe Luce's charge that President Roosevelt 'lied us into war' is not the first time a person named Boothe treacherously assaulted the President of the United States." Drawing on her celebrated wit, Parker was perhaps Luce's most relentless antagonist. One of her most biting comments was that Luce

"would be nice to her inferiors if she could find any." Another old adversary, Vice-President Henry Wallace, made an unprecedented 22 speeches in Luce's district, and on one occasion Roosevelt himself, campaigning against Republican presidential nominee Thomas E. Dewey, stopped off in her district to speak against her.

When the votes were counted on election day, both Franklin Delano Roosevelt and Clare Boothe Luce were reelected. The president had been selected to serve his fourth term by a sizable margin; Luce had barely squeaked by her Democratic opponent.

Luce's assault on Roosevelt was probably the primary reason behind her narrow victory in the 1944 election. Although the chief of state's obviously failing health was a taboo subject in wartime America, Luce had not only talked about it but insisted that electing a dying president was irresponsible. She had become something of a Republican "hatchet"—someone who specializes in attacking party opponents, often at the expense of his or her own popularity. As Wilfrid Sheed noted, "She was still comparatively new at this inflammatory stuff and she fell on it with glee, laying on the irony and woe like a beginning chef at the spice rack."

Shortly after Luce returned to Washington to begin her second two-year term, the House Military Affairs Com-

Luce, whose criticisms of political opponents were likened to "being dynamited by angel-cake," salutes the 1944 Republican convention, where she denounced President Roosevelt.

Writer Dorothy Parker campaigned against Luce during her 1944 bid for reelection. Like many Americans, Parker bitterly resented Luce's attacks on the ailing F.D.R.

mittee, of which she was a member, made an official tour of the battle areas of Europe. They visited London, which was under regular attack from German V-2 rockets, and then France, where they met with General Dwight D. Eisenhower at his headquarters near Paris. The congressional delegation inspected hospitals, spoke with U.S. troops to assess their morale, and saw firsthand the vast amount of military equipment that was being stockpiled for the final battles of World War II. The letters Luce wrote home revealed that she was already beginning to formulate plans for the reconstruction of war-torn Europe. They also show that she thought war hero Eisenhower

might prove a promising Republican presidential candidate once the fighting finally ended.

Sixteen other members of Congress participated in this trip, but from the way the newspapers covered events, one would have thought Luce was traveling alone. The press reported and analyzed her every move and word. This concentrated interest only increased when the other members of the committee returned to the United States for Christmas and she stayed on in Italy to visit the troops of the American Fifth Army over the holidays. She toured hospitals and field positions, talked with countless soldiers, and collected hundreds of names and addresses so that she could report on the soldiers' well-being to their family back home. She returned to America in time to spend New Year's Day, 1945, with her husband.

Luce's trip had spurred her to think about an important topic—postwar relations among the Allies. During the winter of 1944–45, the Allied forces under Eisenhower had liberated Holland and Belgium and were driving into Germany. Soviet forces, meanwhile, were pushing into Germany from the east. Luce correctly anticipated that the war in Europe would end in a few months, when the two arms of the Allied pincers closed on Berlin, the German capital. Then, without a common enemy, the forces of the United States, England, and France

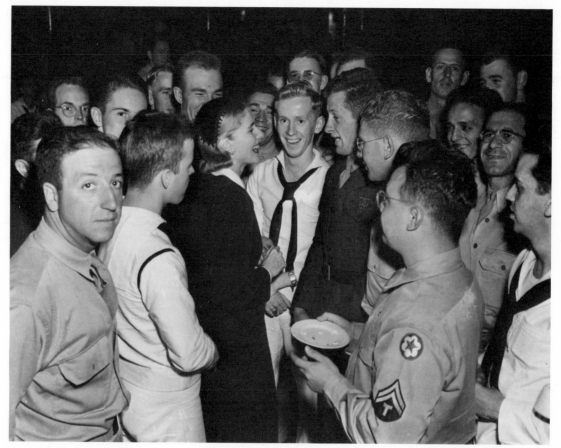

Luce boosts morale during a visit with servicemen. In 1944 she and the rest of the House Military Affairs Committee toured the battle zones of Europe.

would stand arrayed against the Soviets. Luce was certain that the former Allies would compete for territorial control of postwar Europe.

Like many political leaders—her friend Winston Churchill among them—Luce felt that the Soviet Union, though presently an ally for military reasons, posed a great danger to the Western democracies. In her view the United States would have a postwar mission to prevent the spread of communist influence over the European continent. Luce was convinced that the Democrats under Roosevelt either were too sympathetic to the Soviets or simply failed to see the dangers ahead.

World War II finally ended when Germany and Japan surrendered in 1945. That year, *Vogue* called Congresswoman Luce "the country's most controversial woman." According to the

A shaken Luce visits emaciated former inmates of Buchenwald, one of Nazi Germany's most notorious concentration camps. The camp was liberated by the victorious Allies in 1945.

1945 article, her "voting is as contradictory as her independent life, her proposals as creative as her brilliant phrases." Indeed, Luce had earned her reputation as a maverick. Although she was often pegged as a conservative, she had supported several progressive measures, including outlawing the poll tax, a device used in the South to discourage poor blacks from voting. And despite her distrust of communism, she disapproved of the Dies Committee. This group was the fore-runner of the infamous House Un-American Activities Committee, a group that would pursue suspected Communists with all the vehemence—and injustice—of a witch-hunt. ˙

During the time remaining in her second term as representative, Luce lived up to her reputation as a hard worker. She introduced bills to permit profit sharing between owners and workers in industry, to liberalize immigration laws she considered racist, and to promote international cooperation

Leaders (left to right) Churchill, Roosevelt, and Stalin gather at a 1945 conference. Luce distrusted Stalin and feared postwar Soviet expansionism.

to preserve the recently secured peace. A member of the Joint Committee on Atomic Energy, she supported strict government control over the young industry developing peacetime applications of the scientific principles behind the atomic bombs recently dropped on Japan. When, as she had foreseen, the Soviet Union forcibly extended its influence in Eastern Europe, she worked to provide support for refugees from these new regimes. She was also active in persuading Congress to allocate large sums of money toward rebuilding war-torn Europe.

A common thread ran through many of Luce's political positions, from fighting for blacks' right to vote to helping small, war-ravaged countries withstand Soviet domination in the postwar years. As Wilfrid Sheed pointed out in his biography of Luce, despite the wealth and fame she enjoyed during her adult life, she always sympathized with the underdog. He summed up her views in these words: "The

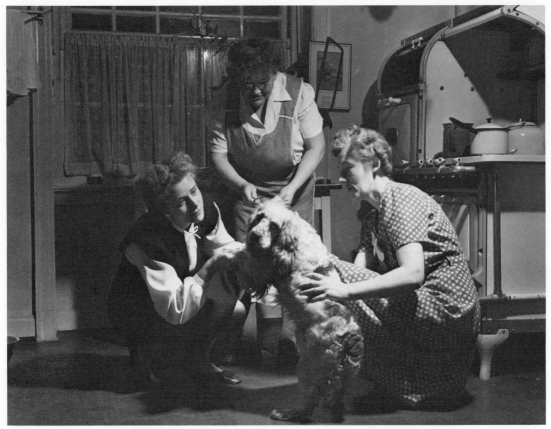

Luce (left) plays with her dog, Speaker—short for Speaker of the House. As a legislator, Luce backed compassionate domestic programs and tough foreign policy.

spunky little guy, with whom she so oddly identifies, must be encouraged to fight the latest bully. If one reason must be adduced for her political career, this is probably it."

As the end of Representative Luce's second term approached, the political scene was changing. Franklin Delano Roosevelt died on April 12, 1945, and was succeeded by Vice-President Harry Truman. Republican party officials pressured Luce to run for a third

term or try for a seat in the Senate. In January 1946 she refused both proposals, stating only that she was doing so for "good and sufficient reasons which will become obvious in time." On February 16, 1946, the reason surfaced: Luce was formally received as a convert into the Roman Catholic church.

Luce's biographers agree that Ann Brokaw's death prodded her mother to undertake a spiritual journey that ultimately resulted in her conversion. A lifelong Protestant, she had never been very religious, but her daughter's death had led her to question her values—and her life. In "The Real Reason," a series of articles published in *McCall's* magazine in the spring of 1947, Luce explained the events that led to her withdrawal from politics and conversion to Catholicism.

These articles are startlingly personal, detailing Luce's anguished state following the death of her daughter and her increasing desperation over the physical horrors and spiritual despair that resulted from World War II. Luce wrote that "all the futile and sterile relationships I had ever nursed or tolerated in pride or vanity, all the lacerations of the spirit suffered so helplessly in contemplating my meaningless world soaked in blood and violence, converged in a vast, sour tide within me." After a series of discussions with Catholic leader Fulton Sheen, she was convinced that his religion would help her understand her daughter's seemingly senseless death and give her life new meaning.

Although her pace slowed a bit, Luce did not entirely drop out of public life after her conversion. She became an active promoter of Catholic causes, traveling widely to speak on college campuses, often at her own expense. In the fall of 1947, she was asked to prepare the screenplay for a movie based on *The Screwtape Letters* by British Catholic writer C. S. Lewis. The

Pope Pius XII conducts a private audience with Clare Boothe Luce. She converted to Catholicism in 1946, the same year she ended her congressional career.

original was a brilliant comedy in the form of letters written between a devil named Screwtape and an apprentice demon called Wormwood. Plans for the film ran aground when Luce refused to alter her script to meet Hollywood standards. Because of this impasse, the project was shelved after three months.

She returned to her spacious home in Ridgefield, Connecticut, a house that one of her guests described as a "Chinese southern plantation." There she turned her attention to a new screenplay, inspired by the true story

Republican president Dwight D. Eisenhower shakes hands with his new ambassador to Italy, Clare Boothe Luce. The 1952 appointment marked her return to politics.

of two French nuns who overcome great obstacles to build a flourishing abbey in America. Luce's screenplay became a successful film called *Come to the Stable*, which was nominated for an Academy Award. In the summer of 1948, Luce was persuaded to speak at the Republican national convention in Philadelphia.

A few months later, Luce received upsetting news: Her beloved brother, David Boothe, had died in an airplane

accident that may very well have been a suicide. Although he was over the age limit, Boothe had been allowed to serve as a pilot in World War II, thanks to his sister's influence. He emerged from the war a hero, but despite Clare Luce's financial and emotional support, he was frequently depressed and unable to hold down a full-time job. In September 1948, he flew his private plane out to sea and was never heard from again. Luce had always stood by her brother, even though he had often disappointed her, and his sudden death came as a blow.

Luce continued to pursue a career as a writer, but she soon found that recapturing her earlier success was a difficult proposition. A play she wrote during this period, entitled *Love Is a Verb*, was turned down by a number of producers and then shelved; her 1951 screenplay for a film to be called *Pilate's Wife* never went into production. Another play, *Child of the Morning*, the story of a young Italian saint who dies while fending off a rapist, was well received by audiences in tryouts in Boston but was panned by most critics and never made it to Broadway.

In 1952, Luce again turned her attention to politics, pinning her hopes for a Republican president on World War II hero General Dwight "Ike" Eisenhower. She joined his campaign and made more than 100 speeches on his behalf across the country. After Eisenhower won in a landslide, he invited her to sit with his family in the presidential box during his Inauguration Day parade. After 20 years of Democratic rule in Washington, a Republican was in the White House. To Luce, it seemed like a good time to get back into politics.

Soon after his election, President Eisenhower asked her to join his administration. The two of them discussed a few positions that she might be suited for, and the president finally asked her to consider becoming the U.S. ambassador to Italy. Foreign policy was one of Luce's greatest strengths as a politician, and she was well acquainted with Italy. The ambassadorship was to prove an excellent choice, both for Clare Boothe Luce and for the Eisenhower administration.

Relaxing on the veranda of her Rome residence, Ambassador Clare Boothe Luce radiates the elegance that led the people of Italy to dub her la Signora, "the Lady."

EIGHT

The Lady

Eisenhower's nomination of Clare Boothe Luce for the post of ambassador to Italy created a furor on both sides of the Atlantic. Her appointment needed the U.S. Senate's approval, and some Democrats felt that Luce's outspoken congressional career disqualified her for a diplomatic post. And although the Italian government, headed by Premier Alcide de Gasperi, officially approved of Luce, many Italians protested that Eisenhower's plan to appoint a woman to the post was both insulting and embarrassing. Nonetheless, after a few false starts, Luce's nomination was confirmed without objection.

In the spring of 1953, 50-year-old Clare Boothe Luce and her husband sailed for Italy, where she would become the first woman ever to occupy a top-rank American diplomatic post.

She was fond of Itay and challenged by the magnitude of her assignment. As ambassador, she would oversee 1,150 employees, 8 consulates, and 9 information centers. Most important, her appointment would enable her to act on her political convictions. As Luce had predicted, postwar relations between the Soviet Union and the United States had deteriorated rapidly while the two superpowers vied with each other to extend their influence into other nations. Italy, a democratic country with a strong Communist party, held a key position in this cold war.

Luce had been in Italy only five months when she attended a September meeting of all the American ambassadors to European countries. The topic that concerned everyone at this gathering was the Trieste problem. Trieste, then a city of about 350,000

Italian demonstrators protest Yugoslavian efforts to claim Trieste. The territorial dispute represented one of the greatest challenges of Luce's diplomatic career.

people, is located at the head of the Adriatic Sea, where Italy and Yugoslavia meet. Because of its importance as a major seaport, Trieste had been fought over for centuries by neighboring countries.

Italy had acquired Trieste after World War I, but following World War II, in which Italy was on the losing side, the territory just across the Adriatic Sea from Italy became the new country of Yugoslavia. Yugoslavia had formed when the population of the area organized under Tito to resist Nazi invaders. Tito's troops occupied Trieste and claimed the city as the Yugoslavs' just reward for their wartime sacrifices. The Italians, meanwhile, insisted that the city was theirs, a claim bolstered by the Italian heritage of most of Trieste's residents.

A temporary solution devised in 1947 designated the city and some of the surrounding area as the Free Territory of Trieste, under the general supervision of the United Nations. The region was divided into two zones. Zone A, in the north, consisted of the city proper and a small parcel of land; it was administered jointly by the Americans and the British. Zone B comprised the remaining, larger land area and was administered by the Yugoslavian government.

After a year, the United States, Britain, and France overthrew the United Nations ruling and recommended that the entire Free Territory be given to Italy. This new arrangement would allow Trieste to benefit from the massive U.S. aid program to Italy.

The American government was now treating its recent World War II enemy Italy as a crucial partner. On the other hand, Yugoslavia, recently a valued ally, was now treated as an enemy. Cold war politics lay behind this dramatic shift in U.S. policy. Despite the strength of its Communist party, postwar Italy had swung to the side of the anticommunist West, while Yugoslavia was now a socialist country within the orbit of the Soviet Union.

The amount of land in dispute was not large, but the passions generated on both sides were intense. After publicly taking a stand, the leaders of both Italy and Yugoslavia would lose face by backing down. When Italian elections were held in June 1953, Premier Alcide de Gasperi was voted out of office. He admitted that he had lost because he had been unable to settle the Trieste issue to the satisfaction of Italian vot-

Yugoslavian communist leader Tito addresses schoolchildren. After World War II, he claimed Trieste as his people's reward for fighting Nazi Germany.

ers. The new Italian government issued loud warnings to Tito and moved troops into the Free Territory to defend its borders. Tito countered by threatening military action.

This was the volatile situation that faced Clare Boothe Luce and the other American ambassadors when they met in the tiny country of Luxembourg in September 1953. The sound of swords rattling was too clear to be ignored; war was now a real possibility. In fact, some observers felt that armed conflict was inevitable. Luce was advised by the other, more experienced ambassadors that there was little point in trying to interfere. "Don't try to solve the

Ambassador Clare Boothe Luce works at her desk. Her reputation as a skillful diplomat was assured after her behind-the-scenes negotiating resolved the Trieste crisis.

Trieste question," Charles Bohlen, the American ambassador to Russia, told her. "It won't be solved short of war."

But Luce was sure that some peaceful resolution of the quarrel could be found if Italy and Yugoslavia were brought together over the bargaining table. Her problem was that as an American ambassador she had no authority to call such a meeting. Diplomats often have very little actual power. Their job is to carry out the policies of their home governments, while carefully avoiding interference in the internal affairs of their host governments.

Therefore, Luce had to draw on all her diplomatic skills simply to promote her solution to the U.S. government. The first step was to bring the matter to President Eisenhower's attention. Luce and her staff tried all the usual channels to engage the president's attention, but they succeeded only when her request was put in the form of an unusual personal note:

Dear Mr. President:
    For want of a two-penny town (called Trieste)
    A Prime Minister was lost (de Gasperi).
    For the want of a Prime Minister
    Italy was lost.

For the want of Italy, NATO was lost.
For the want of Europe, America was lost.
And all for the want of a Two-Penny Town
(called Trieste.)

Luce's warning was heeded in Washington. On Eisenhower's insistence, the Trieste problem was immediately analyzed by his security council, a group that met regularly to advise him on foreign policy. The council agreed with Luce's suggestion that the United States should organize a meeting between Italy and Yugoslavia in some neutral city. The two countries quickly accepted the proposal, which suggests that both sides were war-weary and eager to come to a quick resolution of the dispute. Representatives of Tito and of Giuseppe Pella, the new Italian premier, joined staff members of the British Foreign Office and the American State Department for secret conferences in London.

All went well with the negotiations during the spring and summer of 1954. Meetings were held regularly, and a mutually agreeable solution seemed imminent. Then the Yugoslavian position hardened. Tito's representatives made new demands that were completely unacceptable to the Italians. Luce, reading the reports in her office in Rome, could do nothing. There was even talk that the meetings would break up and that Europe would again be faced with the threat of war over Trieste.

This 1954 cartoon, "The ambassador's new typist," depicts Luce and Premier Giuseppe Pella. It implies that the United States exercised undue influence over Italy.

According to some accounts, Luce learned from her contacts in the Central Intelligence Agency (CIA) that the Yugoslavs were desperately short of wheat because of a series of bad harvests. She reasoned that they might very well be willing to soften their position on Trieste if the United States—which had an enormous surplus of wheat—were to ship some to Yugoslavia. News about the wheat shortage and the possibility of a deal reached the White House. Soon afterward, two things happened: On October 5, 1954, the Yugoslavs and Italians signed a Memorandum of Agreement settling the Trieste problem by giving Italy dominion over the city and Yugoslavia control over much of the surrounding peninsula; three weeks later, a shipment of 400,000 tons of American wheat was unloaded in Yugoslavia.

Details of this agreement—and Luce's role in it—are sketchy. For diplomatic reasons, everyone concerned denied that there had been any deal between the United States and Yugoslavia. It would hardly do for Tito to admit to the Slav inhabitants of Trieste that he had in effect traded their city for some wheat. Nor did the U.S. government want to admit that it had given tons of grain to a communist nation. As a result, Luce was never credited for the important part she seems to have played in settling the Trieste crisis.

Luce did not receive public recognition for her diplomatic coup, but her reputation in foreign policy circles was now assured. She was regarded as a brilliant ambassador with a firm grasp of the realities of European politics. Her admirers in Italy—and she had millions—fondly referred to her as *la Signora*, "the Lady." At the age of 51, she seemed an obvious candidate for higher office.

But at this high point in her political career, Luce began to suffer from a battery of odd physical complaints. In the summer of 1954, the second year of her tenure as ambassador, she began to notice that her right foot was becoming too numb to move, her hair was falling out, and her fingernails were so brittle they cracked. She was chronically fatigued, and the more she rested the more exhausted she felt. Worse still, she reported "seeing things," claiming that she had spotted a huge flying saucer in downtown Rome.

Physical examinations were unable to pinpoint the cause of Luce's troubling symptoms. Her puzzled doctors suggested that she take a long rest back in the United States—and when she did this, in August 1954, it seemed to do her good. Her hair stopped falling out, her teeth no longer felt loose, and the terrible fatigue was gone. But when she returned to Italy to resume her busy schedule, the symptoms began again, now worse than before.

Further tests at the U.S. Naval Hospital in Naples revealed the startling truth: Clare Boothe Luce was being poisoned. Small quantities of arsenic, a deadly toxin, had accumulated in her body. Luce was shocked by the diagnosis and horrified when she was asked whether someone close to her might want to murder her. The CIA was brought in to investigate. The search focused on the ambassadorial residence—a palace on the outskirts of Rome—and was finally narrowed down to the small room she had been using as a bedroom. Investigators found that lead dust containing arsenic had been falling from the painted roses that adorned her ceiling.

Although she had been inhaling this poison nearly every night for 20

Luce rides through Venice in a gondola. In Italy, she again proved she had what a reporter termed "the unpredictable habit of success."

months, her doctors thought that she would recover. An ailing Luce left Italy to recuperate in the United States. The full story of her strange illness was not released for another year, when *Time* ran it under the apt title, "No Bed of Roses."

Luce returned to her duties in Italy, but her enthusiasm diminished as she grew increasingly disillusioned with what she considered "weak" American foreign policy toward the Soviet Union. A crisis that began in October 1956 heightened her discontent.

The Soviet Union had occupied the nation of Hungary after World War II, installing puppet leaders who followed policies dictated by the Soviet government. On October 28, 1956, Imre Nagy, the country's former premier, led a revolt to free the country from communist rule. Hungary's Communist party secretary, Erno Gero, appealed to the Soviet Union for aid in crushing the uprising. On November 4, 200,000 Soviet troops stormed the center of the revolt, the Hungarian capital of Budapest. Luce followed the rebellion's progress from her office, only an hour's flight from Budapest. She sent dozens of messages back to Washington appealing for aid or even a simple statement of support for the Hungarian people. No help came. Neither the United States nor the European democracies stepped in, although she was convinced the Soviet attack could have been stopped if the Western powers had taken a firm stand against it. But with few arms and no help from the outside, the Hungarian rebellion was swiftly crushed by Soviet armed might.

Luce resigned from her diplomatic post a few weeks later. It seems likely that her disappointment over America's failure to support the Hungarian rebellion was a key factor in her decision. The official reason for her departure, however, was health concerns: She still had not fully recovered from the arsenic poisoning, and Henry Luce had recently suffered a mild heart attack. Clare Luce hoped that they would both benefit from a more leisurely lifestyle.

Yet when Luce returned to Washington, the city was abuzz with rumors

Russian tanks burn in the streets of Budapest during the anticommunist Hungarian rebellion. Luce was disappointed when America stood by as the Soviet Union crushed the revolt.

about her political plans. Some specu-
lated that she was about to start a
campaign for the Senate, others that
she would be appointed ambassador
to the Soviet Union. Instead, Clare and
Henry Luce went looking for a home
where they could rest and enjoy some
privacy. In Phoenix, Arizona, they
found a house whose Mediterranean
style reminded Luce of the architec-
ture they had admired in Italy. The
couple settled there, and Clare Luce
occupied herself with a new hobby,
painting.

Still an important public figure even
though she was now semiretired, she
continued to receive more honors than
she could personally accept. The
United States Chamber of Commerce
named her one of the nine greatest
living Americans of 1957. That same
year, the University of Notre Dame
awarded her its Laetare medal, given to
outstanding Catholic men and women.
Two universities, Fordham and Tem-
ple, awarded her honorary degrees.

Although Luce was enjoying her
new, more relaxed life, the idea of a
political career still attracted her. Because of a 1951 constitutional amendment that limited each president to
two terms, Eisenhower could not run
again. His vice-president, Richard Nixon, was not widely popular, even
among Republicans. Sensing that perhaps the time was right, Luce's closest
political supporters began to sound
out party leaders on a daring idea:

*Clare and Henry Luce toss coins in
Rome's Trevi fountain in 1956, the year
she resigned because of health concerns
and her disillusionment with U.S. policy.*

Perhaps Clare Boothe Luce should become the Republican candidate for
president in the upcoming 1960 election. But in February 1959, Luce's life
took another unexpected turn when
President Eisenhower suggested that
she become the new U.S. ambassador
to Brazil. The nomination plunged her
into the last—and most bitter—battle
of her political career.

The trouble arose when the question
of Luce's appointment went before the

Luce displays one of her mosaics. After her return from Italy, she settled down to a quiet life in Arizona, where she devoted much of her time to art.

Senate. Because she had proven herself an able diplomat during her stint in Italy, gaining Senate approval seemed a mere formality. But the nomination encountered heated resistance led by Democratic senator Wayne Morse. Henry Luce's *Time* magazine had been highly critical of the Oregon senator in the past, and many political observers theorized that this was the reason for his strident opposition. Morse and his supporters attacked Clare Luce on all fronts: Her honesty, her reliability, and her past record all came into question. According to one newspaper account, Morse even pumped her doctor for details about her mental health.

Morse's attempts to discredit Clare Luce in the Senate were a failure: Her appointment was approved by a vote of 79 to 11. Still smarting from his stinging attacks, a victorious Luce told a reporter that she was "grateful for the overwhelming vote of confirmation in the Senate. We must now wait until the dust settles." But her next statement did little to encourage any dust settling: "My difficulties of course go some years back when Senator Wayne Morse was kicked in the head by a horse."

These were fighting words, but Luce soon realized that although she had won the confirmation battle she had lost the war. As head of the Senate Subcommittee on the Affairs of the American Republics, Morse would have the power to thwart her efforts in Brazil. Given their past relationship, Luce suspected he would do so. She sent a letter of resignation to Eisenhower, saying that "the climate of good will was poisoned by thousands of words of extraordinarily ugly charges against my person and of distrust of the mission I was to undertake." Shaken by her public battle, 56-year-old Clare Boothe Luce retired from politics.

Seeking greater privacy, Luce and her husband left their home in Phoenix to settle on a ranch in the Arizona countryside. The couple's careers had often separated them in the past, but retirement restored the intimacy of

The Luces relax in a Spanish café during a 1962 vacation. Henry Luce died of a heart attack five years later.

their relationship. According to author and journalist Marie Brenner, Clare Luce once remarked to her husband, "Oh, Harry, you are married to an old, old woman." "Yes," Henry Luce answered fondly, "but I am married to a beautiful old woman."

For the first time in 30 years, Luce dropped out of the public eye. Ceramics, painting, writing, and occasional scuba diving expeditions were her primary pursuits. She wrote short pieces and columns for *Life*, *McCall's*, and other publications, but she stayed out of the limelight. Throughout the 1960s Clare Luce generally stayed away from politics, although a host of government officials sought out her opinions on matters such as foreign policy.

In March 1967 she and her husband were finishing plans to move into a new home in Hawaii when Henry Luce died unexpectedly of a heart attack. Clare Luce buried him alongside her mother and daughter at the Luce estate in Mepkin, South Carolina, which she had donated to an order of Trappist monks. She was deeply saddened by the loss of her husband, a sorrow that must have been compounded because she now had no immediate family left.

This 1980 photograph shows Luce with some political allies. Left to right are Secretary of State Henry Kissinger, Senator Alphonse D'Amato, and writer/publisher William F. Buckley.

Refusing to give in to despair, Luce built and moved into a luxurious home in Hawaii, but her description of her life as a "fur-lined rut" bears testimony to the occasional bouts of loneliness she suffered there. Politics still provided Luce with an escape from this "rut," and she spent a good deal of her time in Washington, D.C. During the 1970s she served under Richard Nixon on the President's Foreign Intelligence Advisory Board (PFIAB), a group that evaluated the work of American information-

gathering operations around the world. She was joined on this committee by such political luminaries such as Nelson Rockefeller, John Connolly, and Henry Kissinger.

Luce was now called the "grand old lady" of Republican politics, and honors continued to pour in during the 1970s and 1980s. These included Congress's Distinguished Service Award and the highest honor that West Point confers on a civilian, the Sylvanus Thayer Award. Luce found the latter tribute especially gratifying because she was the first woman ever to receive it. Two months before her 80th birthday, President Reagan awarded her the Presidential Medal of Freedom, the highest civilian honor bestowed by the U.S. government.

Although Luce joked that old age had "sneaked up on me in the most contemptible way," she remained fit and active to the end. She swam and exercised every morning, and one of her biographers, Sylvia Jukes Morris, remembers the elderly Luce "running along the corridor like a gazelle." When Morris first met Luce in 1980 she noted that "her hair was dyed pale blonde, her face was a classic oval, her skin was moth's-wing fine, almost translucent, and her limpid blue eyes were alternately steely and vivid with intelligence." During the same period, Wilfrid Sheed mused that "a great old age is her least controversial achievement, and it somehow validates her others. Enduring, staying on her feet to the end, seems to be part of her proposition, her wager with Fate."

A typical day for Luce during the 1980s centered on telephone calls and meetings with journalists and politicians. She continued to read voraciously, primarily political reports and books about history and current events. In 1981, Republican president Ronald Reagan reappointed her to the PFIAB.

In 1987 Luce learned that she had a brain tumor. According to the Trappist abbot of Mepkin, she accepted the news stoically, aware that "she was at the realization of a conclusion." After she discovered that the radiation treatments she was receiving were not destroying the tumor, she hosted a dinner for 30 of her closest friends and relatives. Most of her guests realized that the gathering was a farewell party, but Luce joked and chatted with her guests as if nothing was wrong. She was determined to go out with style.

Luce died less than three months later, on October 9, 1987. She was buried at Mepkin in a small private ceremony held by the Trappist monks who lived there. A week after her death, a memorial service was held in New York City's stately St. Patrick's Cathedral. Cardinal John J. O'Connor officiated at the mass, and political columnist William F. Buckley gave the eulogy. The mourners included former president Richard Nixon, chief delegate to the United Nations Vernon Walters, and CIA director William Webster.

Near the end of her life, Clare Boothe Luce, a woman who had accomplished so many "firsts" for her sex, told Wilfrid Sheed that she envied Sandra Day O'Connor, the United States's first female Supreme Court justice. She told Sheed, "I don't want to *be* her. I would just like to have had that kind of chance."

But Clare Boothe Luce had not missed many chances during her life-

Luce prepares for an ocean dive. Her retirement from public life enabled her to pursue many hobbies, including one of her favorite pastimes, scuba diving.

time. Her career had been a remarkable succession of one stunning achievement after another. She was one of the leading magazine editors in the country, an important playwright, an outstanding foreign correspondent, a distinguished member of Congress, and a major figure in international diplomacy. Throughout, indomitable idealism, courage, and stubborn independence characterized her public life.

Clare Boothe Luce certainly owed her success to her many talents. But none of her achievements would have been possible without her self-confidence and sheer determination to break new ground. Perhaps Wilfrid Sheed summed up her life and career best: "She was the first, cutting her way through a man's world that most women were scared even to enter, and making clearings for others in the future. Whatever one feels about the results, it was a colossal undertaking, and Clare's Bowie knife, her tongue and her wits, belong in whatever Hall of Fame is appropriate."

Clare Boothe Luce died on October 9, 1987. Time *magazine eulogized the writer, editor, and politician as "the preeminent Renaissance woman of the century."*

FURTHER READING

Brenner, Marie. "Fast and Luce." *Vanity Fair*. (March 1988):158–82.

Hatch, Alden. *Ambassador Extraordinary: Clare Boothe Luce*. New York: Holt, 1955.

Kobler, John. *Luce: His Time, Life, and Fortune*. Garden City, NY: Doubleday, 1968.

Luce, Clare Boothe. "The Real Reason." *McCall's* (February 1947): 16, (March 1947): 16, (April 1947): 26.

———. *Stuffed Shirts*. Salem, NH: Ayer, 1931.

Morris, Sylvia Jukes. "In Search of Clare Boothe Luce." *New York Times Magazine*, January 31, 1988, 23–33.

Shadegg, Stephen. *Clare Boothe Luce: A Biography*. New York: Simon & Schuster, 1970.

Sheed, Wilfrid. *Clare Boothe Luce*. New York: Dutton, 1982.

Swanberg, W. A. *Luce and His Empire*. New York: Scribners, 1972.

CHRONOLOGY

March 10, 1903	Clare Boothe born in New York City
1913	Her parents, Ann and William Boothe, divorce
1915–17	Clare Boothe studies at the Cathedral School of St. Mary
1917–19	Attends the Castle School, graduating at age 16
1920	Travels to Europe with her mother and stepfather
Aug. 10, 1923	Marries George T. Brokaw
Aug. 24, 1924	Gives birth to her daughter, Ann Brokaw
1929	Divorces George Brokaw
1930	Begins working for *Vanity Fair* magazine
1931	Publishes *Stuffed Shirts*, a collection of satirical essays
1932	Named managing editor of *Vanity Fair*
1933	Works for President Roosevelt's National Recovery Administration
1935	Resigns from *Vanity Fair*
	Serves as European correspondent for Hearst newspapers
Nov. 1935	Begins playwriting career when *Abide with Me* opens on Broadway
	Marries publisher Henry R. Luce
1936	Opening of *The Women*, Clare Luce's first hit play
1938	Luce's play *Kiss the Boys Goodbye* is staged
1939	Luce's drama *Margin for Error* opens
1940	Luce publishes *Europe in the Spring*
1941–42	Travels to Far East as *Life* magazine war correspondent
1943–46	Serves two terms in Congress
Jan. 11, 1944	Ann Brokaw dies in car accident
1946	Clare Luce converts to Catholicism
1948	Writes the screenplay for *Come to the Stable*
1953–56	Serves as U.S. ambassador to Italy
1959	Nominated as ambassador to Brazil; resigns post after a Congressional battle over her appointment
March 1967	Henry Luce dies
1970–87	Clare Luce serves as policy adviser to a variety of Republican politicians, including Presidents Nixon and Reagan
October 9, 1987	Clare Boothe Luce dies

INDEX

INDEX

PICTURE CREDITS

Joseph Lyons, a writer and editor living in Berkeley, California, taught psychology at the University of California for 20 years. A member of the American Psychological Association, he holds a Ph.D. from the University of Kansas and was awarded an honorary degree by the Université de Louvain in Belgium. His books include *People: An Introduction to Psychology, The Ecology of the Body,* and *Psychology and the Measure of Man.*

Matina S. Horner is president of Radcliffe College and associate professor of psychology and social relations at Harvard University. She is best known for her studies of women's motivation, achievement, and personality development. Dr. Horner serves on several national boards and advisory councils, including those of the National Science Foundation, Time Inc., and the Women's Research and Education Institute. She earned her B. A. from Bryn Mawr College and Ph.D. from the University of Michigan, and holds honorary degrees from many colleges and universities, including Mount Holyoke, Smith, Tufts, and the University of Pennsylvania.